Why you shouldn't eat from some white people

THE TRUTH BEHIND WHAT THEY FED US-AND WHY WE'RE STILL HUNGRY

Veronica Pearson

Why you shouldn't eat from some white peopole
Copyright © 2025 by Dammi, Ltd

All rights reserved. No part of this book may be reproduced or transmitted in any form or by any means without written permission from the author.

ISBN: 978-615-46502-9

DEDICATION

This book is dedicated to all of the people that ever believed in good change. My grandmother who always remained strong in spirit up until the day she died. My mother, for always showing a large capacity and fight to love her fellow man no matter whom they were. My Children, Tymir for your constant optimism, Caleb for your unbreakable empathy, and Kiera for the belief that whatever you ask for you can receive. To my BFFs-my gayles, thanks for always knowing what I need even when I don't and to my true friends and family who hold me down, run with me or show me a better way, much love.

Beloved, there is nothing you can do today to make God love you more, and there's nothing you can do to make Him love you any less... Beloved, it's not enough that you know that God loves everyone. You need to know and believe that He loves *you*, and let that revelation burn in your heart, especially when you fail." (p.300-1) Joseph Prince, Destined to Reign

TABLE OF CONTENTS

Introduction 9

Part I: Awakening

Chapter One Who's You? Who's Us?........................... 13
    When identity is fractured, community is fantasy. Until we know who we are, we won't know who to build with.

Chapter Two Women Set The Tone............................. 23
    The emotional thermostat of the home, the community, and the culture—starts with her.

Chapter Three Dead Men Walking............................... 31
    When survival replaces purpose and the walking dead wear Black skin.

Part II: Ancestral Reckoning

Chapter Four Our Ancestors Died For What?............... 39
    From the Middle Passage to medical apartheid, their sacrifice demands our seriousness.

Chapter Five Why Should We Care About Africa 47
    Africa isn't a costume or a campaign—it's our compass. Reconnection is reclamation.

Part III: Cultural Identity

Chapter Six Why Not Address The N Word 57

We cannot build dignity while defending dehumanization.

Chapter Seven I Am Not My Hair Or Am I......................93
    Crowned in shame or crowned in glory? The war over Black women's hair.

Chapter Eight Stop Dressing Up The Fat..........................105
    Body positivity or denial? Health, culture, and the cost of looking good while dying.

Chapter Nine Black People Make Things Popular, White People Make Them Profitable...121
    Cultural theft, economic gatekeeping, and the case for Black ownership.

Part IV: Psychological Truths

Chapter Ten Marriage Is For White People.................... 93
    Untangling generational pain, covenant vs. contract, and love as resistance.

Chapter Eleven Black Racist 102
    When we mirror the systems meant to destroy us. Colorism, hierarchy, and self-hate unpacked.

Chapter Twelve Are You A House Negro Or A Field Negro . 112
    How slave mentalities shape modern behaviors, politics, and proximity power plays.

Part V: Community Struggles

Chapter Thirteen Daddy's Gone But Mommy'll Be Back 121

The ache of abandonment and the illusion of strength in our broken households

Chapter Fourteen Your Child Can't Read Because Of You.... 129
Literacy as liberation, and how generations are perishing without it.

Chapter Fifteen Black Men Left Black Men Behind............ 137
Brotherhood broke. Healing starts when we stop mistaking survival for support.

Chapter Sixteen In The La La Land Of Us Never Integrating 145
How the fantasy of inclusion stripped us of ownership, pride, and community.

Chapter Seventeen The Government Doesn't Care
Because You Don't.. 153
From civic apathy to systemic control, why silence equals suffering.

Part VI: Healing & Responsibility

Chapter Eighteen Stop Investing In Depreciable People......... 160
You can't build legacy by rescuing those committed to sinking.

Chapter Nineteen Extinction 171
Not just of bodies, but of values, vision, and victories. This is a warning, not an obituary.

Notes... 179

INTRODUCTION

Many people will read the title and see the cover of this book and form misconceptions. They might think this is a book about hating the white man or lecturing blacks. All I ask is that you read it not just with an open mind, but with an open heart, because that organ controls your emotions and actions.

The title of this book came to me nearly a year after I thought about the book. As I formed chapter titles and thought about what I wanted to discuss in the book, it hit me, kind of in the fashion of Microsoft Windows 7 commercials, when the idea hits them. But the subject matter came to me from thoughts about my mother one night last year. She had been dead for about six years, and I started thinking about growing up with her: the way she was, the people she was around, and her response to everything. My mother was one of those people that could beat the crap out of you and give you the shirt off her back. She was quiet, but somehow everybody on the street knew her and my aunts and uncles. If someone ever wanted to find them, it wouldn't have been hard. I always was asked, "You sister's daughter?" That's what they called her. I don't know how you get "sister" out of Mary, but whatever.

Her best friend Sandra lived a house behind us with her family. They had known each other for years, so I ended up having her daughter as my best friend in my youth. Sandra and her family were white. These relationships formed a lot of my beliefs and behaviors early in life, and helped me to see and learn things that people who didn't grow up in a mixed neighborhood couldn't learn. One of the lessons was that we can be the best of friends, but our first community, which is our family, influences our beliefs and stays with us for life.

Sandra used to bring my mother food she had cooked all the time. My mother took it and thanked her, but after Sandra left, she scraped the food in the trash, washed the dish, and returned it to her the next day. One time when I was seven or eight, when I asked my mother why she did that, she looked at me and said, "Don't you ever eat from white people." When I asked why, she said, "Either they can't cook or they're nasty." I told my grandmother about the conversation and realized that she taught this to my mother and her parents taught it to her. My grandmother explained how some white people would give them things that weren't good or poisonous, or how they had to watch what they said or did because some white people wanted to hurt black people. Sandra and her family eventually moved from the neighborhood around my third or fourth grade year. By then her daughter Shannon and I had stopped being friends. I'll tell you about that chick later in the book.

As I grew up and talked to other blacks about this, I learned that the majority of them had been taught the same thing. One lady told me how they were the first to integrate a neighborhood, and that her white neighbor gave her kids sandwiches one day. When they came home and told her, she thought it was a goodwill gesture, but when they opened the sandwiches, the meat was rancid. She confronted the woman with a knife, not caring about the consequences, telling her not to give her kids anything else, and that she was a sick person. She also told me stories of whites giving them something, saying it was out of kindness, but they would come back for favors, as if they owed them. And, of course, the story that they couldn't cook, their food would be bland; you know how we love to kill ourselves with seasoning, they let their animals in the kitchen. These are just some of the tales I've heard; some are even crazier.

I chose this for the title when I thought about blacks and our place in America and Africa then and now. I thought about all of the things that we are killing ourselves and our communities with, from lack of education, to welfare, to drugs, just to name a few. Then I started to think about white people's role in American history and the part they played in it: its "discovery," slavery, government, etc., or the misconception the majority of white people have that blacks are out to get them because of past relationships and feelings or even realizing that majority of white people are not racist, just ignorant. Putting them together helped me see how both ethnicities are killing themselves and each other. How blacks have destroyed themselves and their legacy with some of the tools that whites gave them, and how whites are killing themselves through their own machinations; white privilege.

When you look at how a lot of government programs have changed from their original standards once more "brown" people—African Americans, Hispanic, Native Americans, ethnic in general—became involved with them, or how certain beliefs have been harbored and nurtured about each other, you can usually trace it back to the "man" or white people. Then blacks would get a hold of it, and sometimes literally kill themselves or their communities with these programs or false ideologies about race.

In this book, we're going to explore our problems and our solutions. Some may want to curse me, laugh, or cry, or see themselves or someone they know. But I guarantee you will walk away with a different mindset about your lives and each other. I want this book to inspire you to change and move. If we don't get rid of the hate, indifference, and blame that we put on each other, we are going to continually wake up and not know what happened to us or our children.

Side note: I don't generalize when I'm speaking on a subject. So, no these subjects don't pertain to all black people or all white people, etc.

CHAPTER ONE
WHO'S YOU? WHO'S US?

"When you don't know who you come from, you'll confuse survival with belonging—and call anybody 'we' that smiles in your direction."

Veronica Pearson

Every morning I wake and I love whom GOD has made me. I'm not talking about what we have made ourselves into, but what GOD brought us into this world as.
I have never once wanted to look like any other ethnicity. No matter what society, media, or individuals would tell me is better, I learned the strength behind every characteristic of being a Black person or Black woman and loved them all.

There is nothing more exotic than us. From the melanin hue of our skin, no matter the shade, that protects us from aging and helps us soak up the strength of the sun.
To the set and world-dominant color of our eyes that gives us better peripheral vision and absorbs longer and shorter light wavelengths.
To the wideness of our features; our noses that allow us to breathe and circulate air better for optimal cell function—making you move faster, think quicker. The full lips that release more heat in warmer temperatures, create larger erogenous zones, and fuel stronger social interactions.

Muscles designed for endurance and strength. Hips for optimal birthing and balance. Glute muscles for better balance and shock absorption when we walk and run.
Hair that can be styled in countless ways, endure what others can't, and is uniquely ours.
And to the history that shapes us; the good and the bad.

Me expressing this is not saying I am better than anyone else. Me saying these things shows you why I am excellent at being me—why I've learned some will try to make you feel inferior for who you are and what you have, while quietly copying it.

Remember who you are. Perfect the way you are.

Love,
Veronica

The Illusion of Unity

We love to shout, *"We need Black unity!"* — but who is "we," really? On social media, in protest chants, the word sounds powerful. But press people on who's included in that "we" and the answers get hesitant. The truth? We don't even know who we are, much less who we're willing to unite with.

We say we want community, but we don't trust our neighbors. We say we love Blackness, but question the Blackness of anyone who doesn't dress like us, talk like us, vote like us, worship like us.

We fracture ourselves with colorism, classism, religion, politics, and education. We carry internalized racism so deep we don't see the wound anymore. It shows when we dismiss dark skin as less attractive, call educated speech "talking white," critique Black businesses harder than we do others, or hold lighter eyes in higher regard than wider noses.

WHY YOU SHOULDN'T EAT FROM SOME WHITE PEOPLE

We call it "preference," but it's often just the residue of trauma. And until we name it, we can't heal it.

What's in a Name?

Names carry power. Are we Black? African American? Negro? Colored? Moor? Nubian? Israelite? Afro-descendant? We've been called — and called ourselves — all of these. Some were forced on us, some reclaimed, some adopted without knowing the full story.

"Negro" was a European classification meant to dehumanize. "Colored" turned us into a passive noun. "Black" was reborn in the Civil Rights and Black Power era — not just as a color, but as a political declaration: *Black is Beautiful.*

"African American" rose in the 1980s, meant to reconnect us to a stolen origin — but how do you claim African identity when your last name is the name of the person who once owned your ancestors?

James Baldwin said, *"What one cannot speak of, one cannot bring to consciousness."* If we can't speak our true names, we risk living under labels chosen for us by others.

Neighborhoods, Nicknames, and Narratives

Where you're from shapes you — but it's not the sum of you. Some of us inherit trauma by geography: born into housing projects meant to contain us, schooled in buildings that discipline more than educate, surrounded by corners that lure our boys into early graves.

Even within one city, we split ourselves — East side vs. West side, uptown vs. downtown — and make enemies of people who live five blocks away. We hold on to nicknames from childhood that lock us into old identities. "Lil Man" at 40 is still seen as "Lil," no matter how grown he is.

Neighborhood is context, not destiny. We have to stop mistaking location for legacy.

Family Trees with Broken Branches

Before we were "Negro," before we were "Black," we had names and histories tied to tribes, languages, and spiritual meaning. Slavery didn't just steal bodies; it stole identities.

This is why some cling hard to movements like the Hebrew Israelites, the Moors, Pan-Africanism — searching for a root that feels like home. But even DNA tests can't give you the songs, the stories, the ceremonies. Numbers on a chart aren't connection.

Africa Isn't a Costume

Africa is not a dashiki in February or a Wakanda fantasy. It's a continent with depth, complexity, innovation, and living history. Slavery severed our connection, replaced "tribe" with "race," "language" with "labor," "spirituality" with "survival."

To know ourselves fully, we must know our roots globally. You are not just from Mississippi; you are from Mali. Not just Baltimore; from Benin.

Division by Design

White supremacy used divide-and-conquer globally — pitting Caribbean against African American, Afro-Latino against African. We inherited shame and mistrust. We gatekeep each other's Blackness.

WHY YOU SHOULDN'T EAT FROM SOME WHITE PEOPLE

But the truth is, whether we speak Creole, Patois, or Spanglish, we share rhythm, resilience, and ancestors who refused to die quietly.

The Color Line Within

We say "Black people" like it's one shape, one sound, one belief system — but the truth is, we are a spectrum of skin tones, accents, religions, and lived experiences. We're not a monolith, but too often the world treats us like one — and sometimes we start believing that ourselves.

Media flattens us into stereotypes: the thug, the single mom, the athlete, the comic relief, the wise elder. And some of us unknowingly start playing those roles, thinking that's all we can be.

The danger comes when we start policing each other's authenticity. You're not "Black enough" if you read Baldwin or bell hooks, if you can't braid hair, if you grew up in the suburbs. That's not culture — that's trauma disguised as a membership card.

The Eggs & Grits podcast said it best: *"Blackness is not a costume. It's a consciousness."* It's not how you perform — it's how you understand yourself within a legacy that existed before America was even a thought.

If we can't love all versions of us, how can we expect anyone else to?

Cultural Currency and Media Programming

While we're debating identity, the media's already decided who we are — and that image? It's curated. It's not accidental; it's engineered.

Reality TV rewards dysfunction. Music contracts push violence over vision. Viral moments spotlight ignorance because ignorance sells. And the more we consume it, the more it becomes normal. Repetition turns into reality.

We're cultural trendsetters — our music, our slang, our style — but too often, we don't own the platforms or the patents. We make things popular, but we rarely make them profitable.

Representation matters, but representation without responsibility keeps us trapped in the same narrative loop. If the only images of us are pain, poverty, and prison, then our "we" becomes defined by struggle instead of possibility.

We have to tell our own stories — not just in barbershops and kitchens, but on the big screens, in boardrooms, in publishing houses. Ownership of the narrative is ownership of the future.

Trust Issues and Collective Healing

Let's be real — our trust muscles are weak. History made sure of that. Enslavers pitted house against field, light against dark, man against woman. The crack epidemic turned neighbors into enemies. Today, betrayal is just digitized — cancel culture, online beefs, public pile-ons.

Healing those fractures means talking about colorism without shame. It means addressing misogynoir — the way Black women are disrespected even in our own communities. It means making space for Black men's vulnerability. It means standing with our LGBTQ+ family without using scripture as a weapon.

Healing isn't cute or quick. It's hard. It's uncomfortable. But if we don't heal internally, we'll replicate the same harm inside the "liberated" spaces we're trying to build.

The Price of Disconnection

WHY YOU SHOULDN'T EAT FROM SOME WHITE PEOPLE

When we don't know who we are, we build everything — relationships, businesses, movements — on shaky ground. Disconnection breeds hyper-independence, where "I got mine" replaces "We got us."

It's not just emotional. It's economic. If we don't trust each other, we won't buy from each other. We won't bank together. We won't invest together. And that's exactly how systems built to exclude us keep winning — because we keep outsourcing our needs to them.

Unity scares the status quo because unity means strategy, shared resources, and legacy. But unity doesn't come from vibes. It comes from vision — and vision starts with truth.

Reclaiming Our "We"

So how do we move from fractured to whole? It starts with radical self-examination. You can't build "we" if you don't know who "you" are.

We need to redefine community. Sometimes tribe is blood, and sometimes tribe is chosen. The point is, tribe is intentional.

We also have to normalize repair. Disagreements will happen, but conflict can't keep ending in cut-offs. We've mastered shade, but not restoration.

And we have to decide what we're passing on to the next generation. Are we giving them pride, roots, and vision — or just trauma in designer clothes?

Your Reckoning Tools — Chapter Closeout

Reflection Prompt: What part of your identity have you been avoiding, suppressing, or judging? What would it take to love that part?

Accountability Check: Write down three beliefs you hold about other Black people. Now ask yourself — did you learn that from truth or from trauma?

Watch/Read: Find a podcast episode, documentary, or book this week that celebrates a part of the Black diaspora you've ignored or misunderstood. Sit with it.

Action Step: Reach out to someone across a "division" — an elder, someone from a different region, someone of a different faith — and ask them how they see Blackness. Listen without judgment.

Mantra: *I define me. I build we. I remember who I am and reclaim who we were meant to be.*

WHY YOU SHOULDN'T EAT FROM SOME WHITE PEOPLE

🐦 Reflection & Growth

If you had to explain this page to a child, what would you say?

_____

_____

_____

_____

What part of that explanation feels hard for you to admit?

_____

_____

_____

_____

What change can you commit to making today?

_____

_____

_____

_____

CHAPTER TWO
WOMEN SET THE TONE

Each of us has that right, that possibility, to invent ourselves daily. If a person does not invent herself, she will be invented. So, to be bodacious enough to invent ourselves is wise."

Maya Angelou

The Soul of the House Starts with Her

You can walk into a room and feel it before a word is spoken — the shift in air, the energy in the walls. The house might be spotless, the lights on, the dinner hot on the stove, but if the woman in that house is carrying heaviness? The whole place starts to hum off-key.

Black women — whether in a one-bedroom apartment or a family estate — set the tone. In the house. In the family. In the community. In the movement. In the man.

But here's the hard truth: too many of us are leading on fumes instead of fullness. We're building from brokenness and calling it strength. We're pouring from cups that have been empty for years. And when we fall apart, everything we've been holding together falls with us.

VERONICA PEARSON

Think back: Big Mama didn't just serve meals. She stirred stability into every pot. Aunties didn't just gossip on porches — they passed down survival codes between braids and laughter. Even when the man was gone, her presence anchored the home.

But the world has shifted.

Black women are tired. Tired of being the glue without being allowed to be glass. Tired of being called "angry" when we're really exhausted. Tired of "holding it down" while everyone else gets to be soft, scared, and supported. And in that fatigue, some of us have grown numb, cold — not because we stopped caring, but because we've never been allowed to breathe without being needed.

Power in Design — Biology Don't Lie

In nature, the female is often the strategist. The lioness hunts. The eagle chooses only the strongest mate. The female praying mantis can take out her partner mid-act if she deems him unfit. This isn't about cruelty — it's about discernment.

Black women, too, have that power to guide, to choose, to shape outcomes. But when that power is misused or misunderstood, chaos spreads. And when it is stewarded well, it can realign entire households, even nations.

From Eve influencing Adam in Eden to Black women shifting the political landscape in modern elections — we have always been more powerful than the world is comfortable admitting. Sometimes that influence has been used to our own detriment, but when it's used with clarity, it becomes generational alignment.

Big Mama Wasn't Born — She Was Built

WHY YOU SHOULDN'T EAT FROM SOME WHITE PEOPLE

Big Mama didn't come here fully formed. She was forged — by pain, by sacrifice, by staying when she wanted to leave, by loving even when she was wounded. She learned how to set the tone not from a book, but from life handing her no other choice.

She was the thermostat, not the thermometer. She didn't just respond to the atmosphere; she created it. One look from her could stop foolishness before it started. Her hands could bless or break habits.

Fast forward to now — modern women are expected to be Big Mama and Beyoncé at the same time. Soft but strong. Modest but sexy. Provider, nurturer, peacekeeper, therapist. And all while being told we're "too much" for simply feeling too much.

In that juggling act, many of us have lost the intentional art of tone-setting. We've become reactive. We snap instead of speak. We shut down instead of standing firm.

What Energy Are You Leading With?

Tone isn't just about your voice — it's about your presence. Your spiritual climate. Your leadership style. Are you leading with love, or are you leading with defense?

A woman's internal state will mirror in her external environment. If she's at peace, the house flows. If she's burdened, her children carry that tension. If she's spiritually dry, even her prayers sound like complaints. But when she's healed? That woman becomes an altar — a place where life happens.

Proverbs 14:1 says, *"The wise woman builds her house, but with her own hands the foolish one tears hers down."* That's not just about bricks and boards — that's about spiritual architecture.

Economic and Cultural Tone-Setting

Black women aren't just emotional thermostats; we are economic engines. Nielsen reports show we control over $1.5 trillion in spending power and are starting businesses at faster rates than any other demographic. Politically, culturally, socially — our influence is unmatched.

Yet we are still the most disrespected and the most burdened. Our tone must be chosen intentionally — not dictated by trauma. Because when a Black woman chooses her tone, she shapes not only her family's future, but her community's.

Silence Is Not the Standard

Some confuse tone-setting with silence, submission, or suffering for the sake of "keeping the family together." That's not tone — that's trauma wrapped in tradition.

Setting the tone means standing in your purpose, refusing to let chaos have the final say. It means knowing your worth so deeply that you won't shrink for anyone.

God didn't create Eve to be Adam's punching bag. He created her to be his partner. From Sarah to Esther to Deborah to Ruth — women have shifted history through discernment, courage, and strategy.

We've Been Lied To About Strength

The "strong Black woman" label has been both a crown and a cage. It celebrates our resilience while excusing our mistreatment. Society loves our culture, our style, our bodies — but not our boundaries.

We've been told femininity is about appearance. But real femininity is power under pressure. It's knowing when to rest and when to roar. It's healing your bloodline without losing yourself in the process.

WHY YOU SHOULDN'T EAT FROM SOME WHITE PEOPLE

Pop culture has shown us glimpses — Issa on *Insecure*, the women in *For Colored Girls*, Beyoncé's *Lemonade*. All different narratives, but each woman eventually says: *I can't carry this alone. I want to be whole again.*

Healing Is a Lifeline

Motherhood is where tone shows up first. If the mother is rushed, the child grows up anxious. If she's resentful, the child internalizes rejection. If she's numb, the child grows cold.

We've been told to feed them, clothe them, pray for them — but not how to hug them, apologize to them, teach them emotional regulation. Many of us are raising children inside our own unhealed wounds.

We have to stop passing down pain like it's an heirloom.

Depression Wears a Headwrap Too

Black women are 60% more likely to experience depression than white women, but far less likely to seek help. Not because we're stronger — because we've been taught to suppress. We hide our breakdowns behind smiles. We spiritualize our sadness.

Sisterhood is our survival. From sororities to Sunday brunch crews to group chats — we've created spaces to say, *"Sis, I see you."* Encouragement is tone-setting, too.

Not All Men Are the Enemy

We must acknowledge — not every man is harmful. Some want to lead, protect, and love — but our pain can blind us to their presence.

And we must admit that sometimes *we* are the ones who bring toxicity into relationships — through unhealed father wounds, insecurity, or control masked as care.

Accountability isn't just for men. Power without healing becomes poison.

Use the Power or Lose the Legacy

Setting the tone is about intentional choices: deciding that chaos has no home here, that joy is present at Sunday dinner, that affection is abundant, that respect is mutual.

From the moment you wake up, you are the atmosphere. Walk into a room asking: *What am I carrying today? What am I allowing?*

Because whether you have children or not, you are mothering something — a vision, a generation, a nation.

Your Reckoning Tools

Audit Your Atmosphere: Look at your home, relationships, and routines. Do they reflect peace or survival? List what needs to shift.

Daily Check-In: Ask yourself each day, *What tone did I set today? Was it peace, power, or pain?*

Use the Egg Wisdom: Like a human egg choosing viable sperm, choose viable relationships, opportunities, and environments.

Rebuild Sisterhood: Speak life into another Black woman this week. Accountability and love must co-exist.

Rest Intentionally: Schedule joy and softness like you schedule work.

WHY YOU SHOULDN'T EAT FROM SOME WHITE PEOPLE

Teach the Girls Early: Let young girls know they are thermostats, not thermometers.

Mantra: *I am the atmosphere. I am the rhythm. I set the tone on purpose.*

🪶 Reflection & Growth

Where in your life are you already living this truth?

_____

_____

_____

_____

Where are you ignoring it?

_____

_____

_____

_____

What's one way you can bring alignment?

_____

_____

_____

_____

CHAPTER THREE
DEAD MEN WALKING

> "A nation or civilization that continues to produce soft-minded men purchases its own spiritual death on an installment plan."
> Martin Luther King Jr.

WAKE UP.

At some point, we stopped being alive. Not in body — but in purpose, in accountability, in spirit. We started walking like dead men. Still breathing. Still moving. But no light behind the eyes. We laugh, scroll, and make it to Friday. But truthfully? We hollow. Loud on the outside, lost on the inside. Not a little lost — I mean wandering, numb, detached from who we are and what we were sent here to do.

The system knew what it was doing. It's easier to herd the living dead than people who know they have power.

I first heard the term *dead man walking* when I was a kid watching one of those gritty prison dramas. A man was being walked down the hallway to his execution, and the guards shouted it so everyone knew to clear the way. You don't mess with a man who's already on death row. He has nothing to lose.

That phrase stuck with me. But now I hear it every time I scroll past another Black boy killed, another woman buried, another father sentenced. I hear it when the news drops numbers like body counts — casual. I hear it when I see Black people accepting crumbs, still trying to survive off narratives that were never meant to feed us.

Dead men walking. That's us.
Because what else do you call it when a people accept conditions so far beneath their divine worth that they no longer even blink?

The Numbers Don't Lie. The Spirit Does.

You see it in the statistics, but you also see it in the spirit. I see it in the eyes of our children — blank and hardened too soon. In fathers who don't know how to stay. In mothers who forgot how to dream. In churches that are packed on Sunday but empty on Monday when it's time to serve. That's death, too.

Right now, Black people make up 12.4% of the U.S. population, but look at the math when it comes to death, disease, and despair:

- Black men are incarcerated at nearly **five times** the rate of white men. More than **1 in 3 Black boys** born today can expect to go to prison if nothing changes. Prison is not a rite of passage — it's a graveyard for dreams.
- Black women are **2.6 times** more likely to die from pregnancy-related causes than white women. We are dying just trying to bring life into this world. The system calls it coincidence. No baby, it's neglect.
- Black families have, on average, **ten times less wealth** than white families. That's not an income gap — that's generational theft. A stolen inheritance.

We Laugh, Scroll, and Die Slowly

WHY YOU SHOULDN'T EAT FROM SOME WHITE PEOPLE

It didn't happen by chance. From redlining to predatory lending, they planned for us not to have anything to pass down. Black youth suicide rates have nearly **doubled** in the last 15 years. These babies are giving up before life even starts. They're tired — and they're only twelve.

When it comes to health, we're still **60% more likely** to be diagnosed with diabetes, **40% more likely** to have high blood pressure, and **twice as likely** to die from heart disease. Food deserts, medical racism, and environmental injustice are killing us quietly every day.

This isn't coincidence. This is conditioning. Spiritual war disguised as cultural trends. And when you believe nothing can change, you accept it. You normalize it. You defend it. You scroll past it. You even make music about it.

Struggle Ain't Culture. It's a Trap.

We blast lyrics that glorify poverty, mock education, and joke about dead homies — with our kids in the backseat. The clips that go viral are the fights, not the building projects. We've made drama more valuable than discipline, clout more desirable than calling, entertainment more important than enlightenment.

We've made dumb sexy. Trauma marketable. Disrespect the new love language. And we've done it so long we don't notice the stench of death clinging to us.

Struggle is not culture. It's what broken systems hand down and broken people normalize. Blackness is not struggle. Blackness is brilliance. But you can't walk in brilliance when you're addicted to dysfunction.

Kill the Dead Man Before He Kills You

I've watched people I love become caricatures of what the media says we are. Girls I grew up with turned into statistics. Boys I once laughed with locked into hustles that ended in prison or death. Some of my own family stuck in a cycle they didn't create but keep feeding.

We come from royalty — builders, warriors, midwives, philosophers, griots, queens. Yet descendants of kings call each other dogs, bitches, and thugs, thinking that's empowerment.

They laid the trap. We keep walking in. They drew the blueprint. We keep building on it. And then we pass it down like it's inheritance. That's why the work isn't optional — it's survival.

You're gonna have to kill the dead man walking inside of you if you want to live.

Now What Comes Next

We're more likely to show up for a game rally than a parent-teacher conference. More likely to repost trauma than organize solutions. More likely to talk about sex than study generational wealth.

It's not that we don't care — it's that we're tired. But tired doesn't mean we get to check out.

The Bible says: *"I set before you life and death. Choose life, so that you and your descendants may live."* (Deuteronomy 30:19) That's not just scripture — that's strategy.

This book isn't here for you to just read and move on. You're going to reflect, journal, question, shift, and act. Because reading is not enough. Wokeness is not enough. Rage is not enough. This isn't a history book — it's a reckoning.

Your Reckoning Tools

WHY YOU SHOULDN'T EAT FROM SOME WHITE PEOPLE

Reflection Prompt: Where in your life are you "dead man walking"? What areas have you given up on that need to be resurrected?

Accountability Check: Write down three habits, people, or beliefs keeping you in survival mode — and what you're willing to do to release them.

Watch/Read: Find one documentary, podcast episode, or book this week that helps you unlearn a toxic narrative you've normalized.

Action Step: Reach out to one Black person in your circle this week. Speak life into them. Ask what they're dreaming about — and really listen.

Mantra: *"I am no longer available for survival. I am built for transformation."*

Don't Confuse Numbness with Strength

We've gotten so used to pain we mistake numbness for strength. Ignoring it doesn't make it noble, and masking it with hustle or God doesn't make it holy. Strength is facing truth, not just taking blows.

Some of us inherited silence — taught to eat pain for breakfast and smile through dinner. So we raise boys who never cry and girls who never trust. We build households that run on resentment and wonder why nobody wants to stay.

But trauma isn't a personality trait. Being broken is not your brand. Silence is not a legacy worth handing down. You may have been born into brokenness, but you do not have to stay there.

Unlearn the Lie, Rebuild the Life

If you've been surviving so long that thriving feels suspicious, you've been lied to. If joy feels foreign, if peace makes you paranoid, if purpose sounds too good to be true — you've been tricked.

We made dysfunction look like culture, struggle feel like identity, mediocrity seem like safety. But real belonging doesn't cost your truth or require you to shrink.

So start unlearning. Audit every belief that keeps you small. Who told you that you weren't enough? That love had to hurt? That leadership was for someone else? That your softness was weakness?

Rip it all up. Underneath those lies is a soul that still remembers its assignment. You don't have to know the whole plan — just believe healing is your birthright, joy is your inheritance, and transformation is your responsibility.

Come Alive Again

You weren't made to be half-dead, half-awake, half-hoping. You were made to live fully — to feel, see, speak, and love again. Not just romantically, but spiritually, communally, purposefully.

Resurrection starts in your daily decisions: how you talk to your children, care for your space, feed your body, and show up for your dreams. It looks like therapy. Drinking water. Saying no. Asking for help. Showing up even when you're scared.

This isn't cute work. It's not quick work. But it's the only work that sets you free.

So if you've made it this far, don't scroll past your own resurrection.
You were never created to just survive. You were called to rise.

WHY YOU SHOULDN'T EAT FROM SOME WHITE PEOPLE

You are not a statistic. You are not a meme. You are not your past. You are not dead.
You're still here. And that means there's still time to come alive again.

🐦 Reflection & Growth

If you did nothing with this truth, what would your life look like in 5 years?

_____

_____

_____

_____

If you acted on it, what could your life look like?

_____

_____

_____

_____

What's the first action that bridges you from here to there?

_____

_____

_____

_____

CHAPTER FOUR
OUR ANCESTORS DIED FOR WHAT?

Now I see the importance of history, Why my people be in the mess that they be, Many journeys to freedom made in vain,
My brothers on the corner playing ghetto game, I ask you Lord why you enlightened me, Without the enlightenment of all my people
He said 'cause I set myself on a quest for truth, And you was there to quench my thirst, But I am still thirsty...
Arrested Development "Tennessee"

Our Ancestors Died for What?

There's a weight that comes with knowing your people bled for freedoms you now casually scroll past. A heaviness in realizing that some of us treat the ballot box like an option, not a mandate. That we treat education like a hustle instead of a birthright bought with blood.

Our ancestors' fight wasn't abstract. It wasn't a metaphor. It was bruised hands and broken bones, lynch mobs and jail cells, water hoses and dogs. It was Harriet Tubman walking miles through cold swamps with a shotgun, not just to lead people out but to keep them from turning back. It was the Greensboro Four sitting at a Woolworth's counter, enduring spit and slurs and fists so the next generation could order coffee in peace.

The problem is, when history becomes a highlight reel, you forget that each frame was someone's lifetime. You forget that the march from Selma to Montgomery was 54 miles of blistered feet, tear gas, and fear — not a 30-second clip with background music. You forget that our elders didn't march for hashtags; they marched for laws that would keep us alive.

And now, too many of us act like those laws are optional.

The Fragility of Progress

Here's the hard truth: gains are not guarantees. The Voting Rights Act didn't end voter suppression — it just changed its outfit. Integration didn't dissolve racism — it just made it less socially acceptable to say out loud.

Every right we have can be undone. Ask women in America what happened to Roe v. Wade. Ask any Black homeowner what a housing appraisal looks like when the family photos are on the wall versus when the white neighbor "kindly" offers to stand in for the walkthrough. Ask a Black business owner about loan approvals compared to their white counterparts.

We think progress is permanent because we've confused symbols with systems. A Black president doesn't dismantle white supremacy. A Juneteenth holiday doesn't guarantee economic equity. A few celebrities in luxury fashion campaigns don't mean the industry suddenly loves Black designers.

Our elders knew the fight was never over. We've got to remember that.

Economic Battles They Couldn't Finish

WHY YOU SHOULDN'T EAT FROM SOME WHITE PEOPLE

When we talk about what our ancestors died for, we often reduce it to voting or integration. But much of what they wanted was economic power — land, businesses, control over our own labor.

After the Civil War, formerly enslaved people were promised "forty acres and a mule." Most never saw it. The few who did often had that land stolen back through fraud, violence, or government betrayal.

Imagine if that promise had been kept. Generational wealth compounds over time. The value of those acres — passed down, developed, invested — would have been worth billions today. Instead, that wealth was transferred to others, feeding the same systems that once enslaved us.

Our elders also built thriving communities: Greenwood in Tulsa, Parrish Street in Durham, Bronzeville in Chicago. "Black Wall Street" wasn't just a nickname — it was proof of what we could build when we invested in each other. But jealousy and white rage burned those communities to the ground, often with the blessing of law enforcement.

The devastation wasn't just physical; it was psychological. It told us that success would be punished. That no matter how well we played the game, the rules could be rewritten overnight.

The Erasure of Our Genius

We are walking around in a country that benefits daily from our ancestors' intellect while pretending those contributions were accidents or afterthoughts. The traffic light, the blood bank, modern refrigeration, the microphone — innovations with Black fingerprints all over them.

Yet, how often do our children learn these names in school? They can name every Kardashian, but not Garrett Morgan. They can recite TikTok dances, but not the story of Henrietta Lacks, whose cells revolutionized medicine without her consent.

This erasure is deliberate. A people who don't know their history are easier to control. A people who think they've contributed nothing will settle for anything.

Losing the Fire

Somewhere along the way, we mistook comfort for freedom. We traded protest signs for corporate job titles. We started believing that proximity to whiteness was the prize — that a gated community and a luxury car meant we'd "made it."

But you can't out-earn systemic racism. No matter how polished your resume, the system still sees your skin before your credentials.

Our elders didn't risk their lives so we could assimilate into someone else's vision of success. They risked their lives so we could define success for ourselves — collectively, not just individually.

And right now, too many of us are squandering that inheritance.

I can continue with **Part 2** of Chapter Four now, which will cover:

- Modern threats to their sacrifices (voter suppression, economic theft)
- The moral debt we owe them
- Closing tools for reckoning

Modern Threats to Their Sacrifices

WHY YOU SHOULDN'T EAT FROM SOME WHITE PEOPLE

It's easy to believe that the worst is behind us because the water hoses are gone and the lynching photographs are black and white. But oppression just updates its software.

Voter suppression doesn't always look like poll taxes anymore — now it's closed polling stations in Black neighborhoods, purged voter rolls, ID laws designed to disqualify, and district maps gerrymandered so thoroughly they choke the voice out of entire communities.

Economic theft doesn't always look like burning down a business district — now it's predatory lending, wage theft, property tax hikes that push out Black homeowners, and development "revitalization" projects that mysteriously exclude the people who lived there first.

Even our culture is stolen, repackaged, and sold back to us at a premium. Hairstyles that get a Black woman sent home from work suddenly become "boho chic" when worn by a white influencer. Streetwear birthed in the Bronx is "discovered" in Paris. And the same slang our elders used to scold us for gets remixed for Super Bowl commercials.

This is not coincidence. It's a strategy — to strip away ownership and sell back the image without the equity.

The Moral Debt We Owe

We like to say "we're our ancestors' wildest dreams," but I'm not sure that's always true. Dreams require discipline. They require care, consistency, and sacrifice. Our elders didn't just want us to survive — they wanted us to thrive, to hold power, to protect each other.

That means we owe them more than nostalgia. We owe them results.

We owe them community organizations that don't just exist for photo ops but for policy changes. We owe them businesses that hire and mentor our own before anyone else. We owe them classrooms where Black children see themselves in the textbooks and the teachers. We owe them art that speaks truth, even when it's not profitable.

And we owe them the courage to hold each other accountable — to call out the ways we self-sabotage and sell out. Because every time we let fear, apathy, or greed guide our actions, we hand the opposition an unearned victory.

Carrying the Fight Forward

The fight isn't over — it just looks different now. It's not just marches in the street; it's showing up at zoning board meetings when a developer tries to gentrify your block. It's learning the tax code so you can keep your grandmother's house instead of losing it to a cash buyer. It's running for school board so your child's curriculum doesn't erase their history.

The fight is also deeply personal. It's teaching your children who they are before the world tells them who they're not. It's mentoring the young brother who's about to make a choice he can't take back. It's supporting Black-owned businesses even when Amazon offers next-day delivery.

Our elders fought in the ways they could with the tools they had. We've got more tools now — technology, capital access, global communication — but without the same urgency, those tools are just toys.

The Consequences of Forgetting

When we forget what was sacrificed, we lose more than memory — we lose direction. We start believing lies about who we are and what we can achieve. We mistake representation for liberation, consumption for ownership, survival for success.

And that's when the cycle repeats. The same systems our grandparents fought find their way back in — stronger, subtler, and harder to fight because we've grown too comfortable to notice.

History doesn't just repeat when people forget; it repeats when people get lazy. When we stop voting in midterm elections. When we stop holding officials accountable after they've been elected. When we scroll past news of injustice because it's not trending anymore.

Every time we disengage, we dishonor their struggle.

Tools for Reckoning

1. **Audit Your Contribution** – Ask yourself: in the last 12 months, how have I actively moved my community forward? If you can't name three things, start now.
2. **Educate Beyond School** – Build your own curriculum for your household. Your children need to know more than what's in the state-approved textbooks.
3. **Practice Economic Defense** – Buy Black, bank Black, and teach others how to protect and grow their money.
4. **Protect the Vote** – Register early, check your status, and volunteer to get others to the polls.
5. **Mentor Relentlessly** – Take someone under your wing the way someone once took you. Legacy is built in the handoff.

Our ancestors didn't endure what they did so we could treat liberation like a lifestyle brand. They died believing we would build on their work, not just admire it from a distance. The question is — when the next generation asks *us* what we did with the sacrifices we inherited, will we have an answer worth giving?

Reflection & Growth

Who in your life needs to hear this?

_____

_____

_____

How will you bring it to them?

_____

_____

_____

What action will you model so they see it lived, not just spoken?

_____

_____

_____

CHAPTER FIVE
WHY SHOULD WE CARE ABOUT AFRICA

"...my point is that the only authentic identity for the African is the tribe...I am Nigerian because a white man created Nigeria and gave me that identity. I am black because the white man constructed *black* to be as different as possible from his *white*. But I was Igbo before the white man came."

Chimamanda Ngozi Adichie

They Colonized Her. We Romanticize Her. But Few of Us Invest in Her.

Let's stop pretending we don't know why we've been kept from Africa—it was strategic. While we were taught to fear the continent, white nations and global superpowers were quietly claiming pieces of it.

Between 2000 and 2020, China invested over **$155 billion** in African infrastructure—roads, railways, ports, energy plants—while the U.S. lagged behind in both commitment and cultural respect. Meanwhile, Black Americans hold **$1.8 trillion** in annual spending power (Nielsen, 2023), yet less than 2% goes to Black-owned businesses—let alone African ventures.

We post about the beauty of Senegal, wear Ankara prints from Shein, and stream Afrobeats—but rarely channel that energy into partnerships, ownership, or even visits. We celebrate the continent in spirit while abandoning it in practice.

Africa holds the world's largest reserves of gold, diamonds, chromium, and manganese. She's the top cocoa source for the world's chocolate and home to the cobalt that powers our phones. Yet global media still paints her as a beggar, not the bank. This keeps us powerless—the same systems that built their wealth off African soil made sure we'd never think to claim what was ours.

The Divide That Keeps Us Powerless

We don't talk enough about the fractures in the global Black community—African Americans, Africans, Afro-Caribbeans, Afro-Latinx. Instead of moving as one, we clash like competitors.

A Nigerian might say, "Black Americans are lazy." A Jamaican might say, "We had to hustle—no handouts." A Dominican might say, "I'm not Black, I'm Dominican." Black Americans might mock accents or assume Africans live in huts. And white supremacy? It just watches—because that was the plan all along.

The lie wasn't only that Africa was poor—it was that we were separate. In schools, Africa appears small on distorted maps, sending a subconscious message: *she doesn't matter.* In truth, Africa can hold the U.S., China, India, most of Europe—and still have space.

As Ngũgĩ wa Thiong'o said:

"Colonialism is not satisfied merely with holding a people in its grip and emptying the native's brain of all form and content. It goes further: it fills the empty brain with the colonialist's images."

Fractured Images, Edited Memories

Most Africans raised outside the U.S. didn't learn Black American history beyond what Western textbooks allowed. Many were told we were lazy, criminal, ungrateful—just as many Black Americans were only shown starving children, bloated stomachs, and dirt roads when they saw Africa.

We were fed half-truths by full systems.

When all you get is an edited version of someone's identity, mistrust is easy. The Caribbean child grows up proud but misinformed. The African American child grows up dislocated from unspoken roots. The Afro-Latina child is taught to deny her Blackness. The African child in America is mocked for traditional clothes or accent.

In school, my view of Africa came from *Roots* or *Shaka Zulu*. No mention of the Moorish influence on Spanish architecture, Ethiopia's ancient Christianity, or Timbuktu's universities. Africa was erased—on purpose—because if you knew the truth, you'd stop running from your reflection.

The Africa We've Yet to Experience

For many Black Americans, the closest we've been to Africa is through Netflix, Wakanda daydreams, and Tems at brunch. We'll watch *The Woman King* and wear waist beads without knowing their origins.

But how many of us have researched Ghana's dual citizenship? Rwanda's tech revolution? Black American–led real estate projects in Senegal and South Africa?

During Ghana's 2019 "Year of Return," over 1,500 Americans applied for citizenship—most were *not* Black Americans. The initiative was marketed to us, meant for us—but when deeds were signed, we were missing from the room.

Meanwhile, Africa leads in mobile banking, clean energy, and urban innovation. The West shows mud huts, not Kigali's spotless streets or Nairobi's coding hubs. If you saw her fully, you'd stop begging for crumbs in America and start building your own table on ancestral land.

Not Just an Opportunity—A Birthright

Africa is not a trend—it's a birthright. Land is sacred. Community is collective. Marriage is covenant. Elders are honored. These aren't foreign values—they're ours, stripped from us during slavery and colonization.

Our ancestors weren't just taken from Africa—Africa was taken out of us. Yet she still calls. You hear her in a choir's hush, in the sway of your hips to a beat no one taught you, in Sunday head wraps, in protest chants, in spice jars, lullabies, and laughter.

"When the roots are deep, there is no reason to fear the wind."

We've feared the wind because we've forgotten our roots.

Still Chasing Freedom While Using Their Blueprints

We fight for freedom while still measuring ourselves against white systems—wanting their schools, neighborhoods, approval. We want African pride but question Africa's safety. We build Black wealth in U.S. cities but ignore Lagos, Kigali, and Nairobi.

WHY YOU SHOULDN'T EAT FROM SOME WHITE PEOPLE

Ngũgĩ wa Thiong'o calls this the "weaponization of memory." If you control the past, you shape the future's fear. Political manipulation has painted Africa as unstable to justify exploitation.

It's time to write our own maps—ones with our names, our places, our power.

Divided by Design: The Culture Clash That's Killing Ownership

Our conflicts—"too white," "too loud," "too tribal"—are manufactured. Social media profits off cultural beef while others own what we created. Beauty supply stores? Korean-owned. Shea butter? European packaged. Kente prints? Made in China.

Africans own land but lack global platforms. Black Americans shape culture but rarely own production. Both are locked out of industries built on our soil and skin.

Unity would change the global economy. Diaspora migration is happening—families moving to Ghana, building in The Gambia, starting in Rwanda. But without dismantling emotional walls, progress will stall.

The Corruption Myth and What It's Costing Us

"Too corrupt" is the excuse. But is America not? Corruption exists everywhere—it's just more forgivable when it's Western. The U.S. has destabilized African nations for decades, then labeled them unstable.

As of 2023, China's $155B investment dwarfed U.S. and Black American contributions. Waiting for perfection is a trap—Africa was it's own ecosystem before colonizers. Now she needs us to assist in the rebuilding with her and her people.

You Can't Heal While Rejecting Your Roots

You can't claim to love Blackness while rejecting Africa. This is about legacy, inheritance, and becoming whole. Africa isn't broken—she was broken into. Now is the time to reclaim acres and awareness, replacing survival in white systems with ownership in Black ones.

"I am not African because I was born in Africa, but because Africa was born in me." — Kwame Nkrumah

Return to Build, Not Just to Visit

Africa doesn't need pity—she needs partners. The African Renaissance is here: Kiswahili rising as a trade language, Pan-African policy in motion.

Ways to act now:

- Buy real estate in Ghana, Senegal, or Rwanda
- Build co-ops, retreats, or collectives with African entrepreneurs
- Create internships linking U.S. students to African tech hubs
- Learn trade laws and visa pathways
- Study works like *Nile Valley Contributions to Civilization*

America will always find a way to tell us we don't belong. Africa—complex as she is—is the only place where belonging is a birthright.

This isn't nostalgia—it's sovereignty. Not a moment—generations.

Next Steps

WHY YOU SHOULDN'T EAT FROM SOME WHITE PEOPLE

Reconnect, Reclaim, Rebuild

1. Reprogram Your Lens.
Watch how you talk about Africa. Then watch what you consume about her. Replace fly-covered infomercials with documentaries like *Africa: The Great Civilizations* (Henry Louis Gates) and read *From the Browder Files* or *Nile Valley Contributions to Civilization* by Anthony T. Browder. Learn the pre-colonial truths.

2. Reclaim Travel as Strategy.
Get a passport if you don't have one. Plan a trip to Ghana, Senegal, Kenya, or South Africa—not just to sightsee, but to study. Go to a land summit. Meet with a local developer. Touch the soil. Let your vision expand.

3. Invest for Legacy, Not Trend.
Buy land, not just logos. Invest in cacao, textiles, tech startups. Research fair African partnerships. Support African-led businesses and avoid Western resellers who profit from our culture but don't return the dollar.

4. Build Black Bridges.
Create intentional collaborations between African Americans and African diaspora creatives, educators, and entrepreneurs. Make your business global by aligning with someone on the continent. Don't just collaborate with Black people in your city—go worldwide.

5. Teach Our Babies Truth.
Buy maps that show Africa at scale. Put African history in your homeschool, your classroom, or your dinner table. Speak the names of your ancestors. Let your children know they didn't come from slaves—they came from stolen scholars, healers, builders, and warriors.

6. Study Dual Citizenship Options.
Explore countries offering residency or citizenship by return:

Ghana, Sierra Leone, Liberia, Rwanda. Study land laws. Start the paperwork. Long-term power will require mobility.

7. Let Africa Be the Blueprint.
Don't visit her and try to Westernize her. Learn from her. Adapt her values. Apply her wisdom to your business model, your family structure, your spiritual practice.

Final Word:
They showed us flies.
They showed us famine.
But they never showed us gold mines, libraries, architects, or kings.
They lied about her—
So we would forget about us.

No more forgetting.
It's time to go back.
Not just to visit—
But to rebuild.

🐔 Reflection & Growth

What generational pattern do you see reflected here?

_____

_____

_____

_____

How has it touched your own story?

_____

_____

_____

_____

What step can you take to be the one who breaks it?

_____

_____

_____

_____

CHAPTER SIX
WHY NOT ADDRESS THE N WORD

I lived in a plenty tough neighborhood. When somebody called me a 'dirty little Guinea', there was only one thing to do- break his head. When I got older, I realized that you shouldn't do it that way. I realized that you've got to do it through education. Children are not to blame. It is the parents. How can a child know whether his playmate is an Italian, a Jew or Irish, unless the parents have discussed it in the privacy of their homes?
Frank Sinatra

The Swing Set and the Word

I was six years old when I learned that friendship had limits and language could wound deeper than fists. It was a regular South Carolina afternoon—sun out, kids on the playground, dirt on our shoes. Shannon, my white best friend, and I were playing on the swings. She was over at our house so often she was practically family. Her mama was sick, and her daddy would ask my mom to look out for her. My mom agreed, because that's what we do—we take care of people, even when we're the ones overlooked.

That day, Shannon and I got into a small argument—something about who had the swing first. Then out of nowhere, she yelled, "Nigger!"

It hit like a slap. I froze. Six years old, but I knew that word. My family made sure of that. We watched *Roots* and *Shaka Zulu* like they were scripture. I'd seen the chains, the whips, the hatred. And now here was my so-called friend bringing that word to my doorstep, wrapped in childhood innocence and parental silence. We just stared at each other. Her eyes said she knew it was wrong. Mine probably said she had just crossed a line she couldn't uncross. I hit her and she fell to the ground. Then I walked away. I went home, stayed quiet. Shannon would come by the house and I would tell my mom, I not playing with her. She even saw me out one time and told me she was sorry but it didn't matter to me. I didn't tell my mother.until they moved away.

    Looking back, I realize I was protecting my mom because I know how she would go off. Even then I understood the emotional cost—the hurt, the rage, the disappointment. That word held centuries inside it, and Shannon, knowingly or not, threw all of them at me in one swing.

I didn't tell my mama at first. Looking back, I realize I was protecting her. I knew how she would go off. Even then I understood the emotional cost—the hurt, the rage, the disappointment. That word held centuries inside it, and Shannon, knowingly or not, threw all of them at me in one swing.

NIGGA, NIGGA, NIGGA—got it out of your system yet?

For my pigment-challenged people: NIGGER, NIGGER, NIGGER—how does it feel coming out of your mouth?

Maybe you can't say it because it was never planted in you to begin with. Or maybe it's too ingrained to notice. Either way,

WHY YOU SHOULDN'T EAT FROM SOME WHITE PEOPLE

there is no word in the English language that can carry "I love you" and "I'll kill you" in the same breath quite like this one.

Origin Stories

The N-word didn't start as slang—it started as strategy. Its roots trace back to the Latin *niger*, meaning black. On its own, the word wasn't offensive. But after centuries of European colonization, slavery, and racial caste systems, it turned into something poisonous. In Spanish and Portuguese, it became *negro*—still descriptive, but increasingly tied to servitude.

Once it reached American slave owners, it became "nigger"—a verbal branding iron. It wasn't just an insult; it was a tool for erasing identity and instilling inferiority.

You weren't Kwame, Nia, or Adeola anymore—you were just "nigger." A thing. Property. It was the overseer's command, the slave catcher's description, the courtroom's sentence. It was whispered in church sermons claiming God ordained Black inferiority. It was shouted over lynchings. It was the closing word before the rope tightened.

Over time, the enslaved sometimes used the word themselves, because it was the only identity they were allowed to have. Even after Emancipation, the degradation was so familiar that many didn't recognize it as offensive.

Fast forward through Reconstruction, Jim Crow, and the Civil Rights era—the word never left. It just adapted. It hid in jokes, backhanded compliments, and casual conversation.

Leaders like Du Bois, Marcus Garvey, Fannie Lou Hamer, and Martin Luther King Jr. refused to use it. They knew you couldn't build dignity on a foundation of contempt.

So how did we go from rejecting it to defending it?

Short answer: music, media, and money. Long answer: we never fully healed from what the word did to us in the first place.

From Whips to Beats

Today, "nigga" glides through rap verses, comedy punchlines, and casual talk like it's harmless. Jay-Z says, "We took the power out of that word." But did we? Or did we just package the pain and put it on repeat?

Educator Sunni m'Cheaux put it plainly: *"The only racial slurs that ever show up in your sounds are anti-Black."* The N-word has become the soundtrack to our trauma. We nod our heads to it without always realizing the cost.

And capitalism loves it. The music industry, largely run by white executives, profits most when Black artists use the word often. Positive messages rarely get the same promotion.

Think about it: would a Jewish rapper get airplay for saying "kike" every track? Would an Asian comedian build a career around "chink"? No. Because most communities know that reclaiming a weapon built to destroy you is not liberation—it's a trap.

Layers of Damage

Words wire our brains. When we use a word rooted in violence and expect it to carry love, we create cognitive dissonance.

Studies show repeated exposure to negative labels feeds internalized racism—especially in kids. If "nigga" becomes their default label for Blackness, how can they grow up seeing themselves in a light of pride?

WHY YOU SHOULDN'T EAT FROM SOME WHITE PEOPLE

Even if you say it with affection, your brain still holds its history. That's why it feels different when someone outside the culture says it. The trauma hasn't gone—it's just been dressed up.

And spiritually? Words carry vibration. Across African and Caribbean traditions, names are sacred. If you constantly call your brother "nigga," what energy are you really invoking?

Generations Divided

Ask someone born before 1965 about the N-word, and you'll likely get: "We don't play with that." My grandmother said, *"You're not taking back any power—you're keeping it alive for the racist and the weak."*

To elders, the casual use of the word feels like betrayal. They remember when it wasn't slang—it was a death sentence. They remember Emmett Till. They remember the word hanging in the air before the rope was pulled.

That's the gap: they heard it in life-and-death moments; we often hear it in a Drake song. If we want unity, we have to bridge that context gap—and respect the pain that came before us.

Cultural Confusion

White people often ask, "If you can say it, why can't we?" The better question is: why do we want to keep it at all?

I've seen how quickly the word strips dignity. My mother worked decades caring for a wealthy white family. Their daughter—someone who'd eaten at our table and gone to events with my mom—used it on her in anger. My mom had her against the wall before her client begged her to let go.

That's what makes it dangerous: it's a weapon some keep in their back pocket for when all else fails.

Niggas vs. Black People?

Chris Rock's joke—"I love Black people, but I hate niggas"—is more than a laugh line. It's a sign of how deep the word has divided us. We've used it to label parts of our own community as "less than." That's the exact division white supremacy thrives on.

We can't fight racism in the streets and feed it in our speech.

Desensitized but Not Free

The NAACP once held a funeral for the N-word. It didn't stay buried. We haven't grieved what it did to us—we've just gotten comfortable carrying it.

Comfort with oppression is dangerous. The word may not make us flinch anymore, but that doesn't mean it's harmless.

Double Standards and Broken Mirrors

We defend our right to use it, but get furious when outsiders do. That alone proves it still has power. We've turned the mirror into a mask—covering our brilliance with a slur and calling it culture.

The Burden of Legacy

My grandmother, born in the Jim Crow South, told me, *"If you'd ever been called that word while being beaten, you'd never want to hear it again."* She was right.

Our ancestors fought to be called human—not "nigga." Passing the word to our kids like it's a badge dishonors that fight.

Replace. Retire. Reframe.

We have choices:

WHY YOU SHOULDN'T EAT FROM SOME WHITE PEOPLE

- **Retire** it—stop saying it, and don't hand it down.
- **Replace** it—with words that affirm instead of diminish.
- **Reframe**—teach the history so the next generation understands why it's dangerous.

Because words shape worlds. And it's time we built one where this one has no place.

Next Steps
Let's not just walk away from this conversation—let's walk forward. Change happens through intention, community, and truth. We can be the generation that ends the legacy of this word as a cultural crutch. We can choose pride over programming, truth over tradition, and healing over habit. Here are some real, actionable steps to get started:

- **Try to minimize or eliminate the N-word from your vocabulary.** Whether you use it jokingly or affectionately, start replacing it with words that honor who we are. Understand that saying it doesn't take the power back from other races—it only keeps us bound to a mindset we're trying to escape.
- **Find and normalize positive replacements.** If you use the word to show love or frustration, find alternatives that build instead of break. Replace "my nigga" with "my brother," "my sister," "my day one," "my G," or even "my legend." Language can evolve—if we lead the way.
- **Respect others' feelings about the word, especially elders.** Don't be dismissive of those who lived through the era when that word was an open wound. Their silence, their flinching, their disapproval—it all comes from memory. Show them the respect of listening. Let your language reflect your lineage.
- **Teach the youth intentionally.** They aren't lost—they're learning. Let's make sure they're learning the truth. Explain the word's history, from its Latin origins (*niger*, meaning black or brown), to its mutilation in the

American South by people who couldn't pronounce it and didn't care to. Give them stories, not just rules. Understanding fuels transformation.
- **Challenge yourself and your circle.** Have uncomfortable conversations. Be the one who says, "We can do better." Whether you're an artist, educator, parent, or friend—you have influence. Use it wisely.
- **Preserve the word in literature, not life.** Don't erase history—but don't relive it either. Let it live in the books, in the museums, in the documentaries—not in the mouths of our children on playgrounds and social media.
- **Remember that healing is cultural resistance.** Every time you reject the language of oppression, you reclaim something more powerful than a word—you reclaim your name, your lineage, your purpose.

Because we are not what they called us.
We are what we choose to become.
Let the word die, so we can live.

WHY YOU SHOULDN'T EAT FROM SOME WHITE PEOPLE

🪶 Reflection & Growth

What truth on this page hit you the hardest?

_____

_____

_____

_____

How does it show up in your own life?

_____

_____

_____

_____

What one step will you take to shift it?

_____

_____

_____

_____

CHAPTER SEVEN
I AM NOT MY HAIR OR AM I

> Beauty is about perception, not about make-up. I think the beginning of all beauty is knowing and liking oneself. You can't put on make-up, or dress yourself, or do your hair with any sort of fun or joy if you're doing it from a position of correction.
> **Kevyn Aucoin**

The Crown We Were Taught to Hide

There's no conversation more loaded, more ongoing, more rooted in pride and pain, than Black women talking about our hair. It's our crown. It's our inheritance. It's also been used against us—through laws, media, workplace discrimination, and sometimes even by the people who look like us. We've been told it's too much. Too wild. Too unprofessional. Too political. But our hair has never just been about looks. It's been about survival. It's been about spirit.

I remember when I told my ex-husband I was going natural. His response was typical of so many Black men: a confused look followed by, "What? Why?" It wasn't said with cruelty, but with concern—concern rooted in the same conditioning I was trying to break free from. I could tell he imagined I'd walk around looking like Florida Evans from *Good Times*. And as much as I wanted to defend my choice, I couldn't lie—I was thinking the same thing. Would I still feel beautiful? Would my hair look "done"? Society had shaped our beliefs so deeply that even going back to what grows naturally out of our heads felt like rebellion.

But rebellion was necessary. Because what we'd been taught wasn't truth. We had inherited a lie. A lie that said straight was better, more presentable, more acceptable. A lie that told us our hair had to be tamed, altered, or hidden in order to be beautiful. And many of us believed it—so much so that we passed it down to our daughters. We denied them the joy of discovering their real textures, their real selves, before they ever had a chance to embrace it.

This isn't just about hair. It's about the roots of our identity. It's about how we see ourselves and how we let the world define us. It's about the little Black girl who looks in the mirror and questions her worth because her hair doesn't lay flat. It's about the adult woman still battling internalized shame every time she walks into a corporate meeting with her coils unhidden.

Hair is not just style. It's political. It's ancestral. It's emotional. And while we are not only our hair, how we wear it says something about how we see ourselves—and how we want to be seen.

The History in Our Roots

From the moment our ancestors were forced onto ships, our hair became a site of erasure. On the African continent, intricate braids and styles told stories—about tribe, marital status, spiritual beliefs, even one's social role. These styles were passed down like oral history. But when enslavers reached for power, they didn't just strip bodies—they stripped identity. Hair was shaved off, not only for "sanitation," but to sever a cultural lineage.

What was once a crown became a source of control. Black women's hair was labeled "unkempt" or "primitive." Laws like the *Tignon Laws* in 18th-century Louisiana forced Black women to cover their hair in public, an attempt to make them less "attractive" to white men. Ironically, we turned even that into beauty—tying headwraps so boldly that they became statements of resistance.

Generations later, the same policing continued in new forms. Corporate handbooks banned "unprofessional" styles, which almost always meant locs, braids, twists, and afros. Schoolchildren were suspended or sent home for wearing their natural textures. Even now, the CROWN Act—created in 2019 to ban hair discrimination—has to fight for passage state by state. That's how deep this conditioning runs.

The Politics of "Presentable"

Here's the quiet truth: every time we straighten our hair because we "have an interview," every time we warn our daughters about "looking too wild," we're doing the work of white supremacy for them. And it's not always conscious. Many of us survived by blending in. We wanted safety. We wanted access. We wanted the job.

But what is the cost of safety if it comes with self-erasure?

That question has no easy answer. Because for Black women, "presentable" has always been code for "closer to whiteness." That's not a reflection of our worth—it's a reflection of the world we've been navigating.

Internalized Standards and External Pressures

Even inside our own communities, hair has been weaponized. The "good hair vs. bad hair" debate didn't come from us—it came from the system that rewarded proximity to European features. But we kept it alive in playground insults, dating preferences, and family "jokes" that weren't jokes.

I've heard mothers tell their daughters not to swim because "it'll mess up your hair." I've watched women spend hours and hundreds of dollars every few weeks to maintain a look that made them more palatable to others—but left them exhausted and broke. And I've been that woman, too.

This isn't about shaming choices. Wigs, weaves, blowouts—none of these are wrong. The problem is when we feel we have no choice. When we've been so trained to dislike what we see in the mirror that we never even give our natural selves a chance.

Reclaiming the Crown

Choosing to embrace natural hair isn't just about style—it's about reclaiming what was stolen. It's about sending a message to the little girls watching us that their coils are not problems to be fixed, but beauty to be celebrated.

It's also about redefining professionalism, beauty, and self-love on our own terms. It's saying: "I am not here to shrink myself to fit your comfort zone."

And it's a spiritual act. Because our hair, like our skin, is a divine design. Every kink, coil, and curl is proof that we were made with intention. To alter it for survival may be necessary sometimes—but to hide it forever is to agree with the lie that it was never enough.

A Call to the Mirror

The next time you look in the mirror, ask yourself: Are you looking at a style you chose—or one you were told to choose? Are you teaching your children pride—or quiet compliance?

Our ancestors braided seeds into their hair before boarding slave ships, so that no matter where they ended up, they could grow food and survive. That's the power in our roots. Our hair holds history, resilience, and the reminder that we have always made a way out of no way.

We are not just our hair. But how we treat it reflects how we see ourselves.

"I am not my hair. I am not this skin. I am the soul that lives within." — India.Arie

This Crown Is My Testimony

Repeat after me:
My hair is not a mistake.
It is not a problem to solve or a flaw to fix.
It is an extension of my spirit, my culture, my resilience.

WHY YOU SHOULDN'T EAT FROM SOME WHITE PEOPLE

I will no longer shrink myself—or my coils—to fit into anyone's idea of beauty.
My hair does not need to be tamed. It needs to be nourished.
I am not my hair, but my hair is me. And I choose to honor both.

This is about reclamation. Reclaiming our crowns, our culture, and our confidence. No more hiding behind fear or fighting what grows naturally from our scalp. It's not "just hair." It's history. It's protest. It's pride. It's sacred.

You deserve to walk into any room with your head held high— no matter what your hair looks like that day. Because beauty doesn't begin with conformity. It begins with truth. And the truthVERONICA PEARSON

is, your Blackness is not too much. Your hair is not too thick. Your texture is not too hard to manage. Your glory is not too wild. It is divine.

You are divine.

Next Steps

- **Stop letting outside voices define your hair journey.** Learn to care for your natural hair, whether you wear it straight, curly, or coiled.
- **Affirm your crown daily.** Look in the mirror and say: My hair is not "nappy," "messy," or "too much." It is unique. It is powerful.
- **Live your life fully.** Don't skip workouts, vacations, or moments because of your hairstyle. Your life is more important than your leave-out.
- **If you love straight hair,** explore natural silk presses or heat styles that preserve your curl pattern and scalp health.
- **Try transition styles.** Braided weaves, textured wigs, or twist-outs can help ease your journey back to your natural texture.

- **Don't relax your child's hair.** Let her discover her natural self before society tells her to change it.
- **Men—support our journey.** Compliment natural styles. Encourage confidence. Show love without conditions.

Your hair doesn't need permission to be powerful. It just needs you to see it for what it is: a gift. A crown. A declaration.

Wear it proudly.

Reflection & Growth

What emotions did this page stir in you?

_____

_____

_____

_____

How have you seen this play out in your family or community?

_____

_____

_____

_____

What's one action you can take to interrupt that cycle?

_____

_____

_____

CHAPTER EIGHT
STOP DRESSING UP THE FAT

I'm not overweight. I'm just nine inches too short.
Shelley Winters

Buffy's Story: A Hard Truth in a Beautiful Wrap

On September 10, 2018, I watched my cousin Buffy take her last breath. She was 49 years old. We were supposed to be planning her fiftieth birthday celebration. Instead, I sat in a hospital room, playing her favorite gospel music, waiting with my younger cousin Rashad as her body gave up after years of dressing up dysfunction.

The monitor beside her slowed. I glanced at Buffy, then at the screen — and just like that, it flatlined. "She gone," I whispered. Rashad looked at her, then collapsed to the floor. She was more than my cousin — she was like my sister, the glue for much of our family.

Buffy died from complications tied to a fatty liver caused by years of carrying too much weight. That fatty liver developed into cirrhosis, which led to organ failure. Like so many Black women, she denied she was in trouble. "I don't have diabetes. I don't have high blood pressure," she'd say, as though those were the only measures of health. She overlooked other symptoms — swelling, bone and joint pain, skin issues, confusion, exhaustion. Her body had been waving red flags for years. But she, like many of us, dressed it up: hair done, makeup flawless, curves hugged by stylish clothes, serving and giving until nothing was left.

The Dangers of Plus-Size Advocacy

Somewhere along the line, loving ourselves became synonymous with lying to ourselves. The plus-size movement began as a push against body shaming and for diverse beauty standards. But too often, it's shifted from "All bodies deserve dignity" to "Don't hold me accountable to doing better." That's dangerous.

We've mistaken comfort for care, representation for regulation. A snatched waist in a photo doesn't mean your liver is healthy. A confident TikTok dance doesn't guarantee normal cholesterol. Like the dangerously thin runway models of the past, plus-size influencers and entertainers are now being financially rewarded for sustaining bodies that are breaking down on the inside.

The numbers don't lie:

The numbers don't lie:

- In 2011–2012, adult obesity in the U.S. was 34.9%.
- By 2020, it climbed to 41.9%, and it remains about the same today.
- Black adults have the highest obesity rate of any racial group in America — nearly **50% overall**, with historic data showing rates for Black women peaking around **57%**.
- Obesity-related conditions such as heart disease, stroke, type 2 diabetes, and certain cancers remain among the leading causes of preventable, premature death.
- Severe obesity can shorten lifespan by 8–10 years.

Companies profit from this — plus-size clothing lines, shapewear, oversized furniture, bigger caskets, sponsorships, all tied to sustaining the condition. Like the heroin chic trend of the '90s, this is capitalism dressed up as empowerment.

No movement can erase the damage being done inside our cells, joints, and organs.

What the Kids Are Learning

We don't just dress up the fat — we pass it down.

Plus-size clothing for toddlers. Pediatricians prescribing Ozempic to 12-year-olds. A generation being handed a legacy of disease disguised as self-acceptance. It's not their fault — it's ours.

When parents skip doctor's appointments but never miss hair or nail appointments, kids notice. When we reward them with fast food but don't teach them hydration or how to read a nutrition label, they notice. Saying "They're just big boned" or "That's baby fat" is not preserving joy — it's robbing them of future ease.

Obesity is generational trauma in edible form. We're feeding our kids grief we haven't dealt with, and it shows up in their bodies as low energy, early puberty, asthma, anxiety, and shame.

If we want to break the cycle, we have to stop feeding it — literally and figuratively.

When Health Ain't Sexy but Disease Is Dressed Up

Black men and women can make anything look good — even dysfunction. We rock our curves in bodycon, beat our faces while our bodies scream, drip in designer while taking water pills. We've learned to carry trauma with beauty, and the world stopped checking on us.

But you can't sexy away dysfunction. Infertility is rising among Black women — over 32% linked to obesity-related complications. Being "thick" might be a trend, but it's not sustaining us. Our bodies don't care how many likes we get — they care if our organs work.

Relationships suffer too. Pain, shallow breathing, and low energy make intimacy hard. Looking sexy isn't the same as feeling healthy. And for some, the rejection they feel isn't about weight alone — it's about the lack of care for the body being offered for love.

The Strong Black Woman Is Dying Silently

She's the provider, the fixer, the one who prays, pays, and pulls everybody together. She's also the one with untreated high blood pressure, stress-induced insomnia, hormonal imbalances, and chronic fatigue. She's revered in public but abandoned in private — including by herself.

We watched Big Mama cook for the neighborhood while ignoring the swelling in her ankles. We called it love and legacy, but we're burying our women before 60. We spiritualize pain but avoid the doctor. Because we carry it well — no one knows how close we are to collapsing.

Strength must include saying no, asking for help, and loving yourself enough to break the curse.

Our Diet Is Spiritual Warfare

Food was survival during slavery. We turned scraps into soul food, but what once kept us alive is now killing us through overconsumption. Meals designed to sustain forced labor were never meant to sustain long-term health.

WHY YOU SHOULDN'T EAT FROM SOME WHITE PEOPLE

The Black church is no exception. Scripture gives dietary guidance, yet after service we serve fried, sugary, over-salted meals. Pastors preach deliverance while battling preventable disease. If the body is the temple, neglecting it is neglecting the altar.

Sex, Dating, and the Disconnect

Obesity impacts desire and ability in the bedroom. Pain, shortness of breath, and low stamina make intimacy difficult. For men, excess weight can cause erectile dysfunction and physical barriers.

A healthy body supports attraction, performance, and connection. Ignoring that reality creates resentment and broken chemistry.

What Black Men Are Really Saying

When I asked Black men their biggest issue with Black women, I expected attitude or sex to top the list. Instead, many said, "Black women don't work out like other women do."

It's not always about access — sometimes it's about priority. To some men, it looks like we've accepted disease as normal. And whether fair or not, how we show up reflects on the whole community.

We can't demand love and respect while neglecting the vessel meant to carry them.

Discipline Is a Form of Self-Love

Love without discipline is just decoration. Caring for your body is reverence for what God gave you and commitment to those who depend on you.

Choosing health doesn't make you less authentic — it reconnects you to a legacy of warriors and healers. You don't have to be thin, but you do have to try.

Reclaim Movement as Joy

Movement isn't punishment — it's proof of life. Walk. Stretch. Dance. Get sun. Movement is in our blood; it's how we've survived and thrived.

Do it quietly, do it daily, but do it for you.

Your Struggle Is Their Strategy

The plus-size industry is worth over $24 billion. Bariatric surgery, shapewear, oversized caskets — all profiting from our inaction. We are the product.

When you spend more on hair than on health, they win. When you teach beauty but not blood pressure checks, they win. The return for us is shorter lifespans and generational bondage disguised as empowerment.

Live for Them. Really Live.

We say we'd die for our kids. But would we live for them? Buffy didn't get to see her grandkids grow because she ignored warning signs.

Genetics isn't the excuse we think it is. Comparing yourself to someone heavier doesn't erase your own health risks.

You have one body. No spares. It deserves honesty, effort, and care.

Next Steps: Don't Just Change Your Look — Change Your Life

WHY YOU SHOULDN'T EAT FROM SOME WHITE PEOPLE

- Stop normalizing illness.
- Eat smarter: prep fruits and salads, drink more water, add fiber.
- Move more: start small and build.
- Get sunlight.
- Go meatless twice a week.
- Let go of shame; celebrate small wins.

Self-Check Questions:
Can you walk stairs without being winded? Do you have daily joint pain? Are you avoiding intimacy? When was your last physical? If most answers make you uncomfortable, it's time to act.

Final Word: You Can't Dress Up a Dead Body

This isn't about fatphobia or vanity. You can't outdress dysfunction. I watched Buffy — a nurturer and believer — die, not from fate, but from years of ignoring herself.

From here on out, we choose discipline as love. Movement as medicine. Real nourishment as protest.

We refuse to be another beautifully dressed tragedy.

One body. One life. Don't decorate your coffin — defend your life.

Reflection & Growth

What excuses came to mind while reading this?

_____

_____

_____

_____

If you removed the excuses, what would be possible?

_____

_____

_____

_____

What small but bold step can you take toward that possibility?

_____

_____

_____

_____

CHAPTER NINE
Black People Make Things Popular, White People make them Profitable

"Black people create culture, and white corporations cash in. We've been the heartbeat, but never the shareholders."
Killer Mike

What We Birth Gets Bought

Black hands built Wall Street — literally. The original wall that gave "Wall Street" its name wasn't symbolic. It was a 12-foot fortification constructed in the 1600s by enslaved Africans under Dutch colonial rule to protect white settlers' economic interests. Those same laborers not only laid the foundation for the financial capital of the world but were also bought and sold nearby at one of America's first official slave markets. Enslaved Africans were the first and main commodity traded there — before stocks, oil, or any modern symbols of wealth.

America's financial system was built on slavery. Entire national economies, including those of the U.S. and major European powers, were fueled by buying, selling, insuring, and exploiting Black people. We built the street, but we were never meant to walk it — not as investors, not as stakeholders, not even as free people.

Centuries later, economic exclusion continues. Wall Street still profits off Black labor, creativity, and culture — from hip-hop to tech to fashion to even prisons — but the wealth rarely returns to the communities that spark it. Today, to qualify as an accredited investor, you need at least $1 million in net worth or $200,000 annual income for two consecutive years. That's more than a number — it's a gate that keeps us out.

We make the sauce. They bottle it and sell it back to us — with interest.

While learning African-American history, I discovered how inventions like the cotton gin, irrigation systems, and mumbo sauce were created by Black people — many enslaved, illiterate, or denied legal rights — yet stolen, patented, and credited to someone else. I once thought, "They took advantage because our people couldn't read or file paperwork." Now I know it's deeper. Even with degrees, businesses, and legal knowledge, the systems move the goalposts and change the rules to protect their advantage. Institutional theft didn't end with slavery; it just rebranded.

From inventions to TikTok dances, slang, hair trends, and food, Black culture is the engine of cool. The world doesn't move till we move. Yet when the cash registers start ringing, our names are rarely on the checks.

We invented "on fleek." Target sold eyebrow kits. Keara Wilson made the "Savage" dance; Addison Rae got the Tonight Show spot. Video game companies turned Black-originated dances like the Milly Rock into profit-driving emotes without credit or compensation. Our genius gets global; their bank accounts get bigger.

We're the architects of trend and taste, but what we birth is monetized and sold back to us. That's not an accident. That's a blueprint.

WHY YOU SHOULDN'T EAT FROM SOME WHITE PEOPLE

From Jazz to TikTok — The Cycle Repeats

This is about wealth, equity, and ownership.

According to a 2021 McKinsey report, the median wealth of Black households is $24,000 compared to $188,000 for white households. That's not a gap — that's a robbery. One culprit? We create, but rarely own.

We made jazz, but Benny Goodman got crowned "King." We birthed rock and roll, but Elvis got the throne. We sculpted hip-hop, yet white men in boardrooms decide how to market our pain.

Clubhouse began as a digital cookout; when the funding came, it didn't go to the culture. BlackPlanet thrived before Facebook — no billions in funding. Vine birthed Black internet stars — shut down before monetization. TikTok recycled the format, elevated white creators, and cashed out.

We're the launchpad, but we rarely get the stock options. If you don't invest in your idea, someone else will — and they'll profit off the version that erases you.

In music, from Motown to mixtapes, Black sound shaped global culture, yet streaming revenues largely flow to labels and tech companies. Hip-hop is a $10 billion industry, but many pioneers are still broke or fighting for their masters decades later.

This is a cultural heist.

Creators vs. Owners — Who Profits?

Being loved online doesn't mean being paid in real life. TikTok built a $400 billion valuation off Black trends, slang, dances, and voices. Black Twitter gave free PR to brands for over a decade — no equity.

Visibility isn't value. Ownership is. A dance is intellectual property. A meme is modern marketing. But when we don't file the paperwork, lawyers and brands turn us into content, not partners.

Black inventors held fewer than 1% of U.S. patents from 2000 to 2016 — not because we weren't creating, but because systems were built to exclude us.

In gaming, dances like the Shoot Dance were lifted by Fortnite, helping earn over $1 billion in revenue during its peak, without paying the originators. We're the unpaid R&D department — proving what works, but rarely cashing in.

Fashion, Beauty, and the Black Dollar

From streetwear to sculpted edges, from big hoops to bold prints, everything called fresh or edgy started on a Black block. We made streetwear luxury before "Virgil Abloh" and "Louis Vuitton" were in the same sentence. Dapper Dan turned knockoffs into couture and Harlem into a runway — and got raided for it. Decades later, brands copied his style, then called it collaboration after public outcry.

For Us, By Us wasn't just a slogan — it was survival. FUBU fit our flavor and grossed $350 million annually at its peak. Supreme, drawing heavily from Black aesthetics, sold for $2.1 billion. Black designers still struggle for shelf space and investor backing.

In 2020, Black Americans spent $1.6 trillion — yet only 2% reached Black-owned businesses. In beauty, we dominate demand but rarely control supply. The $2.5 billion Black haircare industry is over 80% non-Black-owned. Even most beauty supply stores serving Black customers are Korean-owned due to decades of capital and zoning barriers.

WHY YOU SHOULDN'T EAT FROM SOME WHITE PEOPLE

The problem isn't innovation; it's infrastructure. We've been conditioned to see quality only when whiteness packages it. Until we own the supply chain, trademarks, contracts, and capital, we'll keep building dreams someone else will scale and claim.

Bodies Built by Us, Profited by Them

Black women's bodies have been policed, ridiculed, and hypersexualized since slavery. Sarah Baartman — the "Hottentot Venus" — was paraded across Europe for her curves. Centuries later, those same features are billion-dollar commodities.

When Jennifer Lopez's curves made headlines, it was called groundbreaking. The Kardashians industrialized the same look Black women were shamed for. The "Brazilian Butt Lift" is rooted in West African features trafficked to Brazil, yet white women profit from the aesthetic while Black women face higher surgery death rates.

Our bodies have been commodified without our consent — from physical features to the "Strong Black Woman" trope used in ads and films while ignoring our mental and physical health costs. Until we reclaim our image, we'll remain the unpaid muse in someone else's marketing plan.

Don't Just Go Viral — Go Viable

Too many of us build momentum without infrastructure. Trademark your name. Register your LLC. Learn licensing, royalties, and intellectual property. If you can name it, brand it, and build it — you can own it.

Black business ownership rose over 30% between 2019 and 2022, but a business isn't just a hustle — it's a legacy machine. The average Black dollar leaves our community in six hours compared to 17 days in the Asian community.

Spend and collaborate intentionally. Partner with other Black vendors, manufacturers, and designers. Build ecosystems, not just audiences. If you can influence culture, you can lead the market.

Build the Table — Don't Beg for a Seat

Stop waiting for a seat at someone else's table. Issa Rae built from YouTube to a media empire. Tyler Perry turned plays into the largest Black-owned studio in the U.S., built on former Confederate land.

Your name is currency. Protect it. Paperwork is power. Shop Black. Bank Black. Hire Black. If you can't find a Black-owned option, create it or help someone else do it.

Legacy Over Likes

Cultural capital is our inheritance. Legacy is built through structure, discipline, and intergenerational strategy. Teach the next generation ownership. Show them that culture is currency.

As Charlamagne Tha God said, "Black people make things hot. White people make it a business." The blueprint is in our hands — we just have to use it.

We are not just the wave. We are the ocean.

Next Steps: Turn Culture Into Currency

1. Audit Your Influence

- Ask yourself: What trends, language, products, or content do I promote with my dollar or platform?
- Write down 3 brands you constantly buy or repost. Who owns them? Are they Black-owned or Black-inspired?

2. Replace and Reinvest

- Replace at least one non-Black-owned brand you frequently support with a Black-owned alternative.
- Reinvest in your community — whether that's shopping at Black bookstores, buying from Black fashion designers, or supporting local entrepreneurs.

3. Build and Buy Black — Consistently

- Choose one Black-owned business to support every month.
- Share their story on your social media or tell a friend (word of mouth is still free marketing).
- If you're a business owner, intentionally collaborate with other Black creatives, vendors, and manufacturers.

4. Turn Talent Into Ownership

- Don't just be the face — own the formula, the factory, the funding.
- If you're an artist, content creator, or trendsetter, retain the IP (intellectual property).
- Learn the basics of licensing, trademarks, and brand protection.

5. Educate Yourself on the Business Side

- Read books like *PowerNomics* by Dr. Claud Anderson or *Our Black Year* by Maggie Anderson.
- Watch documentaries like *The Black Godfather*, *The Remix: Hip Hop x Fashion*, or *High on the Hog*.

6. Interrupt the Algorithm

- Stop reposting content that glorifies appropriation without attribution.

- Create content that spotlights Black brilliance, invention, and entrepreneurship.
- Use hashtags like #BlackOwned, #BuyBlack, and #WeBuiltThis — make us trend ourselves.

7. Get Equity or Don't Engage

- If a company uses your culture, your following, or your ideas — ask for equity, not just exposure.
- If you work in a space where Black culture is monetized but Black people aren't compensated, speak up or step away.

8. Collaborate, Don't Compete

- Stop gatekeeping and start group economics.
- Build collectives: food cooperatives, artist unions, investment groups, Black buying clubs.
- Ask: Who else should be eating from this table with me?

9. Teach the Next Generation the Game

- Start teaching children about ownership, copyright, and creativity as capital.
- Use examples like Robert Smith, Rihanna, David Steward, Tyler Perry, and Pinky Cole — not just for celebrity worship, but for understanding the moves behind the money.

10. Call It Out. Cash Out. Create Again.

- When you see cultural theft or watered-down versions of Black creations being sold back to us — call it out.
- Then redirect the energy: cash out by spending or investing intentionally.
- And finally, create: build something better, bolder, and Black-owned from the start.

WHY YOU SHOULDN'T EAT FROM SOME WHITE PEOPLE

🪶 Reflection & Growth

Where in your life are you already living this truth?

_____

_____

_____

_____

Where are you ignoring it?

_____

_____

_____

_____

What's one way you can bring alignment?

_____

_____

_____

_____

CHAPTER TEN
MARRIAGE IS FOR WHITE PEOPLE

Marriage is the union of two divinities that a third might be born on earth. It is the union of two souls in a strong love for the abolishment of separateness. It is that higher unity which fuses the separate unities within the two spirits. It is the golden ring in a chain whose beginning is a glance, and whose ending is Eternity. It is the pure rain that falls from an unblemished sky to fructify and bless the fields of divine Nature.
       Kahlil Gibran

The Lie We Inherited

I wasn't raised to dream about marriage. Nobody sat me down to explain what a wife truly was. The only "rule" my cousins and I heard was: *Don't have babies before you get married.* That was it. No talk about building a life together. No wisdom about choosing someone who protects your peace, not just your body. No real blueprint.

Instead, I saw women survive marriages, not thrive in them. My grandmother stayed with my grandfather through eviction, infidelity, and neglect. She nursed him when he was sick and raised their children while he drank, lied, and disappeared. She thought marriage meant surviving together — even if only one person was doing the surviving.

Some of us grew up watching our moms or other women in our lives — or our fathers or other men — look flat-out miserable in their marriages; from lack of love, lack of money, cheating or abuse (mentally and physically) from both parties. They'd warn us, "Don't get married," and because we were kids, we thought they knew what they were talking about. But the truth is, they didn't know what marriage was supposed to be. They couldn't teach it because they had never experienced it. All they could hand us was the version of love they knew — one laced with disappointment, silence, or survival. And we took their word as gospel, not realizing it was pain talking, not wisdom.

That kind of love looked more like war than partnership. And that war became the model my mom and aunts carried into their own marriages.
So when I say, *"Marriage is for white people"* — I'm not speaking truth. I'm naming the lie we were handed.

What We Were Never Taught About Marriage

In our culture today, we throw around phrases like "Wifey," "I don't need a man," and "He's just simpin'." But those aren't just words — they're shields.

- *"Wifey"* means doing all the work of a wife — sex, meals, loyalty, emotional support — without the honor or covering.
- *"I don't need a man"* usually means, *I'm tired of needing men who don't show up.*
- *"Simp"* is how broken boys insult healthy men who lead with love instead of ego.

WHY YOU SHOULDN'T EAT FROM SOME WHITE PEOPLE

We are loud about independence but quiet about covenant. And that silence has a cost.

According to Pew Research (2021), only **30% of Black adults** are married, compared to 48% of all adults nationally. Over **70% of Black children** are born to single-parent households — not because we're anti-love, but because we inherited broken blueprints.

Our elders told us to avoid pregnancy before marriage. But they didn't — or couldn't — teach us the *purpose* of marriage itself. So now we're navigating love in a culture that glorifies situationships and laughs at commitment... then cries in private when we can't find it.

Celebrity Chaos Isn't Our Blueprint

We've let celebrities model dysfunction for us. One week we're reposting a messy Instagram fight between co-parents; the next week we're shocked at a celebrity divorce.

They market drama as normal. Beyoncé's *Lemonade* became tabloid gossip instead of a study on forgiveness. Cardi B's on-again-off-again marriage was framed as entertainment. Will and Jada became clickbait.

What we don't see as often? The quiet couples who build in peace. Who repair without making it a press release. Who argue and reconcile without cameras.
Those marriages exist — but chaos is what gets clicks. And the more we consume it, the more we normalize it.

The Blueprint of Dysfunction

The phrase "marriage is for white people" became famous in a 2006 *Washington Post* article when a Black boy said it flat out.

People didn't just hear it — they started believing it. And acting on it.

We stopped marrying. We started glorifying endurance over structure, trauma bonding over intimacy. We mistook cohabitation for commitment.

We saw uncles with five baby mamas, aunties who never remarried because the first marriage almost killed them, and couples who stayed "together" only because they couldn't afford to split.

And here's the truth: that legal paper matters. Spiritually, legally, generationally — it is not just a contract. It is a covenant. A covering.

Malachi 2:14 says: *"The Lord is witness between you and the wife of your youth. She is your partner, the wife of your marriage covenant."*

Why White People Get the "Marriage Advantage"

Here's a truth that stings:
White people are taught — in both family and professional spaces — that marriage makes you look stable, trustworthy, and promotable. It's an unspoken rule in corporate America, politics, and even real estate investing.

A married man is assumed to be dependable. A married woman is assumed to be grounded. They get the contracts, the promotions, the business loans. Marriage signals "responsibility" in ways singleness — especially Black singleness — does not.

Meanwhile, in our community, marriage is often framed as a burden or a trap. That cultural difference isn't just about love — it's about economics and power.

WHY YOU SHOULDN'T EAT FROM SOME WHITE PEOPLE

Mental Health Benefits of a Healthy Marriage

We also don't talk enough about the mental health benefits of a good marriage. Research from the American Psychological Association shows that happily married people experience **lower rates of depression**, **reduced stress hormones**, and **longer life expectancy**.

For Black people — living under chronic systemic stress — that kind of partnership can literally be life-extending.
A good marriage offers emotional regulation, accountability, and a safe place to process life. That's more than romance. That's medicine.

And I've seen it — not on Instagram, but in real life.
I've got married cousins who still dress alike after 20-plus years, not because they have to, but because they like it. Friends who share everything — passwords, finances, plans — because trust makes secrecy unnecessary. Couples who are not just in love, but genuinely like each other and look forward to hanging out together. Women I know who out-earn their husbands but still have men who lead their households with strength, vision, and humility — and who don't feel the need to compete with them.

These marriages aren't photo ops. They're living proof that commitment, friendship, and respect can grow over decades. They are the antidote to the propaganda telling us Black love can't last or can't be healthy.

For Black people — living under chronic systemic stress — that kind of partnership can literally be life-extending.
A good marriage offers emotional regulation, accountability, and a safe place to process life. That's more than romance. That's medicine.

Homespun Reality Check

We will spend years holding down relationships that hold us back. You'll see women building whole businesses while a man sleeps in 'til noon, talking about he's "waiting on his big break." You'll see men breaking their necks to pay all the bills for a woman who refuses to work or multiple what's given, but somehow always has money for wigs, nails, and a weekend trip with her girls.

That's not partnership. That's parenthood. And marriage is not supposed to be you raising a grown adult with better shoes than you.

I know sisters who've been "engaged" for ten years — no wedding date, no ring upgrade, no legal anything. That's not commitment, that's a lease with an option to renew.

Unhealed Love Can't Build Legacy

Unhealed people enter marriage looking for rescue, not reflection. They want their partner to fix what their parents broke. When that doesn't happen, they withdraw or attack.

When you've been raised in chaos, peace feels suspicious. That's why so many people sabotage stability — it feels "too quiet."

And this is where the system profits:

- Single mothers juggling two jobs feed an economy that needs cheap labor.
- Fatherless children are more likely to end up in the juvenile and prison systems — which are billion-dollar industries.
- Unmarried couples rent instead of building wealth through home ownership.

Marriage, done right, disrupts all of that. Which is exactly why it's worth protecting.

Marriage Still Works — If We Do

It's not that marriage is broken. It's that the blueprint we inherited was.
We don't need fairy tales — we need functional, faithful, focused partnerships.

We rebuild by:

- Teaching our sons how to be husbands before they become fathers.
- Showing our daughters they are worthy of lasting love, not lingering love.
- Normalizing pre-marital counseling and healing work.
- Choosing partners with vision, not just chemistry.

Black love is resistance. Black marriage is legacy.
It is not for white people. It's for healed, growing, covenant-minded people who want their last name to mean something in 100 years.

Tools for Transformation

1. If it's not covenant, stop calling it commitment.
   Living together for years doesn't equal marriage. If the conversation doesn't include God, goals, and growth, you're not building a legacy—you're burning time.
2. Stop applying to be a wife to someone who hasn't applied to be a husband.
   "Wifey" is a delay tactic. Don't build a family with someone who can't even build a future with you—on paper and in prayer.

3. Normalize pre-marital counseling and healing work. You can't outrun your childhood wounds in someone else's arms. Do the work before you say "I do."
4. Don't let money shame you out of marriage. A courthouse wedding is $50. Love don't need a loan. A wedding is a day. A marriage is the legacy.
5. Teach your children what marriage is and what it isn't. Don't just warn them about sex—teach them about covenant, purpose, emotional intelligence, and the spiritual beauty of choosing someone who's choosing you too.
6. Remember: Black love is resistance. Black marriage is legacy.

Marriage isn't just for white people. It's for Black people who are ready to break cycles, build futures, and love on purpose.

WHY YOU SHOULDN'T EAT FROM SOME WHITE PEOPLE

🪶 Reflection & Growth

What emotions did this page stir in you?

_____

_____

_____

_____

How have you seen this play out in your family or community?

_____

_____

_____

_____

What's one action you can take to interrupt that cycle?

_____

_____

_____

_____

CHAPTER ELEVEN
BLACK RACIST

Let's not hate ourselves. We are all we have. We cannot change anything until we accept that. I cannot do this alone. I don't love myself enough to do it alone, but I can do it if we have a pact, if I am keeping up my end of the bargain. I have been a longtime perpetrator of hate crimes against myself, and I am turning myself in. I have had enough.
Margaret Cho

Opening – David Banner's Truth

I was hosting a community forum years ago in Charleston, South Carolina, and one of the guest speakers was David Banner—if you know, you know. During the Q&A, an audience member asked him a layered question:
How did he feel when something he said didn't get the same attention it would have if a lighter-skinned activist had said it? At the time, Jesse Williams was everywhere in the media.

The audience member wasn't attacking Jesse, but naming a frustration many darker-skinned activists felt. Banner's response silenced the room:

"You want me to be upset at a lighter-skinned man because his ancestors was raped a little more than mine? It doesn't matter

WHY YOU SHOULDN'T EAT FROM SOME WHITE PEOPLE

how the message gets out—as long as the message is getting out. Especially if it's about Black unity."

His answer was raw, layered, and necessary. History shows lighter-skinned Black people sometimes had safer access to platforms—not because they were better, but because white racism saw proximity to whiteness as less threatening. That proximity has always been complicated. But if the goal is collective growth, the mic should matter less than the message—so long as it's amplifying us all.

What We Mean by "Black Racist"

Let's get this straight: Black people cannot be systemically racist.
We didn't build the courts, schools, banks, police, media, tech, or housing policies that decide who gets protected and who gets punished. That's not our name on those blueprints.

But we can still hold prejudice. We can still harm each other. We can still bleed on our own people.

Racism is prejudice plus power—written into laws, policies, and institutions. Prejudice is what we do to each other based on lies we've been taught about ourselves. And that runs deep.

When we say:
"She too dark."
"He too nappy."
"They too ghetto."
That's not white folks talking—that's Black mouths moving with white logic.

We've been conditioned to love a version of Blackness that sits as close to whiteness as possible. That's why the light-skinned girl with Eurocentric features gets the lead role while the dark-skinned sister with braids gets reduced to the "friend." That's why the suburban brother gets labeled "soft" and the one from the trenches gets called "authentic." We sharpened the very tools that were once used to cut us down—and now we use them on each other.

The House and the Field Still Live in Us

On the plantation, skin tone could mean survival. Light-skinned Black people—often the result of rape—were kept in the house, closer to whiteness, closer to food, clothes, and less back-breaking labor. Darker-skinned people worked the fields from sunup to sundown, catching hell for things they didn't cause.

This was by design. White supremacy didn't just chain our bodies—it colonized our minds. Lighter meant better. Closer to white meant closer to safety. Fast forward, and we still play this out:

Light-skinned girl? "Pretty," "marketable."
Dark-skinned girl? "Strong," "intimidating."
Light-skinned boy? "Well-spoken," "safe."
Dark-skinned boy? "Aggressive," "too hood."

We call it "preference," but it's really pain passed down and dressed as taste. You hear it in barbershops, at reunions, even in church. It's poison we keep serving to each other.

Respectability Politics & Media Programming

Respectability politics told us if we dressed, spoke, and behaved a certain way, maybe we'd be "let in." At first, it was survival. But it became a standard—and now we police each other with it.

"Don't wear that hoodie."
"Change your name on the résumé."
"Fix your hair before the interview."

WHY YOU SHOULDN'T EAT FROM SOME WHITE PEOPLE

We've mistaken assimilation for advancement.
And media poured gasoline on that fire. Hollywood gave the world—and us—a script about who we are: the thug, the mammy, the Jezebel, the magical Negro, the angry Black woman. Lighter skin? Love interest. Darker skin? Comic relief or cautionary tale.

Dr. Joy DeGruy put it plain:

"We've been conditioned to believe that everything good is white. So when we look at ourselves, we don't see good."

We didn't write that first draft—but we've been editing it for years.

Gatekeeping & Internal Policing

Too often we act like Blackness is a checklist. If you didn't grow up poor, get jumped, play spades, or "talk a certain way," you get labeled "not really Black." We turn pain into proof of authenticity and exclude anyone whose life didn't mirror our own scars.

Blackness isn't a box—it's a universe. Our ancestors were poets and scientists, warriors and healers. But we still bully the anime kid, side-eye the violin player, and call the coder "weird" for not fitting the stereotype. That's not protecting the culture—it's policing it.

Some Black conservatives, especially those on the far right, have mastered the art of copy-and-paste politics. They recycle the same narrow, baseless talking points that white conservatives have been using for decades—word for word—without ever pausing to examine if those talking points hold any weight when stacked against history, policy, or lived experience. You'll hear, *"Democrats want Black people dependent on the government,"* as if the history of welfare and government aid hasn't also propped up white rural America. You'll hear, *"Republicans follow scripture and biblical principles,"* as if scripture wasn't historically used to justify slavery, segregation, and denying women the right to vote. These lines get passed around like family recipes, except they aren't nourishing anybody—they're choking us.

This isn't about agreeing or disagreeing with every single point of a political platform. It's about knowing when you've traded critical thinking for comfort, nuance for slogans. When you adopt the talking points of those who have historically worked against your progress, you aren't speaking from conviction—you're echoing from conditioning.

Some would argue this is the modern-day "house Negro" mentality—aligning with those who benefit from our oppression for a seat at their table. The problem is, that table was never built for us to eat at. And every time we recite their script instead of writing our own, we're not just misrepresenting ourselves—we're reinforcing the same system we claim to be free from.

Black-on-Black Crime: Mirror, Not Myth

Yes, crime is proximity-based and white-on-white crime exists too. But that doesn't erase the harm we do to each other. Shooting someone over shoes. Robbing a sister who's just as broke as you. That's not "the system" pulling the trigger—that's unhealed trauma with a weapon in its hand.

We can't only say "Black Lives Matter" when the shooter is white or wearing blue. If your trigger forgets that your target is your reflection, you've already joined the system you claim to resist.

The Black Class War

WHY YOU SHOULDN'T EAT FROM SOME WHITE PEOPLE

When some of us "make it," we start talking different, shopping different, and looking down at folks who remind us of where we came from. Success becomes separation.

We shame the EBT mom while forgetting Big Mama fed half the block with food stamps. We act like a degree protects us from racism or a Tesla exempts us from discrimination. We invest with everybody but our own, then wonder why our communities stay underfunded. That's not elevation—that's elitism.

Love, Lust & Anti-Black Dating Preferences

Dating has become another battleground for proximity to whiteness. Swipe left if she's dark-skinned. Swipe left if his name is "too Black." We call it "preferences," but if your "type" consistently excludes people who look like your family, that's not preference—it's programming.

We're all guilty of mistaking aesthetics for alignment, choosing validation over connection. And when your foundation is built on rejecting your own reflection, you can't build legacy—only instability.

The Black Woman: Most Disrespected

Malcolm X wasn't lying when he said the most disrespected person in America is the Black woman. What he didn't add is that the disrespect often comes from inside the house—inside our own communities.

We'll march behind her, let her birth our children, and then call her "too strong" when she survives without us. We'll worship mama but degrade women in our lyrics. We'll sleep with Black women but only show off someone "foreign" in public.

This isn't just misogyny—it's racialized misogyny. And you can't claim to love your people if you don't protect the women who've always been first to fight and last to be thanked.

Turning the Mirror Into Medicine

We didn't invent the poison. But we keep drinking it.
We inherited the dysfunction. But we keep passing it down.

Healing starts with asking why before reacting, educating instead of embarrassing, loving someone even when they remind you of pain you haven't healed yet. Blackness is not one shape, style, or income bracket. It's global. It's divine.

You don't get to revoke someone's Black card because they don't mirror your experience. And you don't get to demand a system value us if we're still devaluing each other.

Healing Begins With Us

It starts with how we speak to each other, who we center, and who we give grace to. If trauma can be passed down, so can healing. You can stop mocking your niece's name, start checking on your brother's mental health, and celebrate every shade and shape in your community.

You might not dismantle the prison industrial complex today, but you can raise a child who loves their Blackness, heal your friendships, and challenge your family. Internalized oppression might not be our fault—but it is our responsibility.

Closing Call to Action

This isn't just a chapter. It's a charge.
Audit your language. Interrupt bias in your family. Expand your love. Mentor beyond your mirror. Celebrate loudly.

WHY YOU SHOULDN'T EAT FROM SOME WHITE PEOPLE

Because if we don't love us—raw, real, fully—then who will?
We are not the enemy. We are the answer.
Let's write the next chapter Black, bold, and healed—by design.

It's not enough to post "Black excellence" if we still practice Black exclusion. It's not enough to clap for Black billionaires if we're still silencing Black barbers, teachers, doulas, janitors, queer kids, and artists. It's not enough to wear black pride cloth in February if we still shame someone for not being "Black enough" in March.

The revolution is internal before it's external.
And the fight for Black liberation starts with us liberating each other—from the stereotypes, from the shaming, from the silent rules we never agreed to but still enforce.

This chapter is titled *Black Racist* not to insult, but to interrupt.
To disrupt the whisper that says you gotta be lighter to be beautiful. Straighter to be smart. Whiter to be worthy.
To confront the lie that says we can't harm what we don't own.
Because harm doesn't need a title. Just a target.
And sometimes, we've made each other the target—on the streets, in the schools, in our own homes.

But if you got this far, you're already different.
You're choosing to see it. Name it. Heal it.

Here's how:

- Audit your language. Who taught you what was "ghetto"? Who taught you what was "beautiful"? Challenge those definitions.
- Interrupt bias in your family. When Grandma shows favoritism based on skin tone or your uncle jokes about a queer cousin—say something.
- Expand your love. Date who you love—but ask yourself why. Examine what you praise and what you avoid.

- Mentor beyond your mirror. Uplift people who don't fit your idea of "respectable" Blackness. Embrace all flavors of the culture.
- Celebrate loudly. Blackness in all forms is worthy of joy, not just survival.

Because if we don't love us—raw, real, fully—then who will?

You are not the slave. You are not the master. You are the rewrite.

And it's time we started editing our story like we know we are the authors.

    Let this be the last chapter we write under their rules.

    Let the next one be Black, bold, and healed—by design

WHY YOU SHOULDN'T EAT FROM SOME WHITE PEOPLE

🐦 Reflection & Growth

If you had to explain this page to a child, what would you say?

_____

_____

_____

_____

What part of that explanation feels hard for you to admit?

_____

_____

_____

_____

What change can you commit to making today?

_____

_____

_____

_____

VERONICA PEARSON

CHAPTER TWELVE
ARE YOU A HOUSE NEGRO OR A FIELD NEGRO

Once you change your philosophy, you change your thought pattern. Once you change your thought pattern, you change your — your attitude. Once you change your attitude, it changes your behavior pattern and then you go on into some action. As long as you got a sit-down philosophy, you'll have a sit-down thought pattern, and as long as you think that old sit-down thought you'll be in some kind of sit-down action.
Malcolm X

The Illusion of Proximity and the Legacy of Division

This isn't just a quote. It's a cultural mirror we've been dodging for decades.
Malcolm X broke it down in 1963, but the roots stretch back further — to the psychological warfare of slavery.

Historically, the "house Negro" lived inside the master's home, wore better clothes, ate better scraps, and sometimes gained the master's trust. The "field Negro" worked sunup to sundown in the fields, under the whip, in the dirt. One had proximity to power, the other proximity to the soil. But both were enslaved. Both were property.

WHY YOU SHOULDN'T EAT FROM SOME WHITE PEOPLE

That's the seed white supremacy planted — not just physical separation, but mental. Proximity to whiteness became mistaken for freedom.

Fast forward to 2025, and tell me you don't see the same thing: In the boardroom. In politics. On social media. At your family reunion.

We still have a chasm between those who've "made it" and those still grinding. Between bougie and broke. Between HBCU grads and street scholars. Between those who code-switch for respect — and those who refuse.

It ain't about class anymore. It's about consciousness.
And the most dangerous Negro?
The one who thinks money, education, or a whiteness-adjacent lifestyle makes them free.

Respectability Will Not Save Us

Today, the house and field dynamic wears new clothes.
It shows up in how we speak, vote, dress, and dream.

Take politics: Some Black folks believe aligning with Republicans makes them more refined, more "above" the struggle. They talk about "pulling yourself up by your bootstraps" like we were ever given boots. Others pledge blind loyalty to Democrats who offer us nothing but symbolism and empty representation. Neither party is our savior — and both are full of Black faces performing for platforms that don't serve us.

In media, we see "safe" Blackness — curated, profitable, palatable — that never challenges white comfort. Loved by the system because it asks nothing of it.

Respectability whispers that if we speak proper, dress modestly, and behave ourselves, we might finally be accepted. But history has already proven: You can have a Harvard degree, a billion-dollar bank account, a white spouse — and still be a "nigger" in this country.

Code-Switching and the Cost of Survival

Let's talk about code-switching — the daily dance of "sounding white" at work and "sounding Black" at home. For many, it's survival. But for some, it becomes performance — a silencing of self. That's the house Negro spirit at work: adapting so deeply to the master's ways that you forget your own.

On the flip side, the field Negro spirit shows up in the community organizer, the co-op founder, the coder teaching kids after school. But here's the truth — this isn't about demonizing one and glorifying the other. Sometimes the house was survival. Sometimes the field was forced. And both roles came with loss.

This ain't about guilt. It's about awareness.
Whose interests are you serving? Whose language are you speaking? Whose freedom are you fighting for?

When Class Becomes the New Chain

Classism is the new whip. You ever see how some Black folks get money and suddenly "those people" can't be around their kids? They move out, talk down, forget the time they couldn't afford gas.

Between 2019 and 2022, median Black household wealth rose 60% to about $44,900 — a big gain, but still a fraction of the median white household's $285,000. The racial wealth gap actually widened by nearly $50,000 in that same period. Over half of Black households remain in the lowest wealth tier.

This is what Dr. Joy DeGruy calls "post-traumatic slave syndrome" — the internalized belief that whiteness is better and

WHY YOU SHOULDN'T EAT FROM SOME WHITE PEOPLE

proximity to it is protection. Straight hair over natural. Ivy League over HBCU. Nordstrom over Nubian. Yoga over Yoruba.

Assimilation is not elevation.
We can't heal while chasing white approval.
We can't build if we're ashamed of our Blackness.
And we can't love each other if we believe some of us are "better" than the rest.

The Algorithm Is the New Plantation

Malcolm X said:
"The house Negro loved his master more than the master loved himself... If the master got sick, the house Negro said, 'What's the matter, boss, we sick?'"

That still stings because it still rings true. Only now, the master's house is a billion-dollar algorithm.
Social media platforms have become digital plantations. Black creators make the culture; corporations own the platforms and monetize it.

Black audiences don't just consume — they convert. Black adults are 71% more likely than average to buy products promoted by an influencer. YouTube reaches 63% of Black adults, and nearly half have purchased something they saw there. Yet countless Black creators have seen their work stolen, erased, or credited to others — because the algorithm doesn't reward origin, it rewards optics.

We are still field Negroes in labor, house Negroes in marketing. And sometimes the "master's face" isn't white — it's us. Because internalized racism doesn't just live in those who hate Blackness. It lives in those taught to dilute it for white comfort and corporate gain.

VERONICA PEARSON

Success Isn't the Problem — Forgetting Is

Respectability politics tells us, *Be less Black and maybe they'll treat you better.* But the system doesn't hate us because we're loud or wear locs. It fears us because a loved us can't be controlled.

"Acting white" became an insult not because excellence is bad, but because whiteness often meant betrayal — forgetting your people. The problem isn't having the degree, the car, the vocabulary. It's when success comes with amnesia.

You can go to Yale and still be down. Drive a luxury car and still build for the hood. The issue is leaving the field and never coming back.

Only 1.6% of Fortune 500 CEOs are Black. Across U.S. companies, just 5% of senior management roles are held by Black professionals. And the number of new Black board appointees is shrinking — down to just 12% of new seats in 2024. That's not equity. That's tokenism with a budget.

The Plantation Didn't Die — It Got Upgraded

Colonial thinking trained us to distrust each other — to divide by skin tone, speech, salary.
Light-skinned girl walks in? She's "stuck-up."
Dark-skinned man with confidence? "Aggressive."
Black person critiques behavior? "Tearing down the culture."

These are all branches from the same plantation tree — and the roots are white supremacy. As long as we're busy measuring "real Blackness," we're avoiding the real truth: None of us were ever meant to win under this system.

Burn the Labels, Build the Future

WHY YOU SHOULDN'T EAT FROM SOME WHITE PEOPLE

Here's the truth: house and field were both enslaved. One had a nicer view, maybe softer hands — but neither was free. Yet we glamorize the house for access, glorify the field for authenticity, and forget the master only cared that we stayed in line.

It's time to kill the category.
The real revolution isn't choosing one side — it's burning down the system that created the sides.

We need the activist and the attorney.
The nurse and the doula.
The rapper and the reader.
The Ph.D. and the freedom fighter.

We need to stop asking, "Are you house or field?" and start asking, "What are you building — and who are you building it for?"

Freedom looks like ownership.
Like policy.
Like land.
Like literacy.
Like love that doesn't apologize for being loud, Black, radical, and revolutionary.

We are not enemies. We are echoes of each other — children of both the cotton field and the blueprint, both the protest and the prayer. The goal isn't to trade places. The goal is to burn the whole plantation down — mentally, emotionally, economically — and build something we own.

Together.

Next Steps: From Division to Liberation

1. **Check Your Position — and Your Posture.**
   Ask yourself: Are you building bridges or fences? Are

you using your access to uplift or to distance? Whether you're in the boardroom or on the block, your positioning should serve our people — not separate you from them.
2. **Call Out Respectability Politics — Gently but Firmly.**
When you hear someone suggest a Black child needs to "talk white" to succeed, or a sister shouldn't wear her hair naturally to an interview — pause. Challenge it. Educate with love, not shame. Freedom starts with truth.
3. **Build Something Bigger Than Your Brand.**
Whether you're an entrepreneur, artist, activist, or 9-to-5 grinder — ask: Who benefits from my success? Start a mentorship circle. Fund a scholarship. Create a lane for someone else. Legacy is communal.
4. **Bridge the Gap Between "Bougie" and "Broke."**
Host a conversation. Bring together folks from all walks of Black life — the professor and the poet, the nurse and the nonprofit worker, the street-smart and the book-smart. We need each other's strategies, stories, and strengths.
5. **Heal Your Colonial Wounds.**
Unpack the beliefs that tell you proximity to whiteness is safety. Journal your earliest memories of feeling "too Black" or "not Black enough." Rewrite them. Then teach your children, your siblings, your circle how to rewrite theirs too.
6. **Honor the Field Work.**
Support grassroots organizers, neighborhood caregivers, and culture-shapers doing work that doesn't go viral but keeps our people alive. Donate, amplify, and show up — not for clout, but for community.
7. **Be the Architect.**
Stop asking where you belong — start asking what you're building. Every meeting, every decision, every room you enter: bring your people with you. In voice, in vision, in value. This system wasn't built for us — so let's build one that is.

WHY YOU SHOULDN'T EAT FROM SOME WHITE PEOPLE

"I'm the architect. I'm here to build us something better."

Because the only thing that matters now is the freedom we're willing to fight for —
together.

🐦 Reflection & Growth

What truth on this page hit you the hardest?

_____

_____

_____

_____

How does it show up in your own life?

_____

_____

_____

_____

What one step will you take to shift it?

_____

_____

_____

_____

CHAPTER THIRTEEN
DADDY'S GONE BUT MOMMY'LL BE BACK

Parents are sometimes a bit of a disappointment to their children. They don't fulfill the promise of their early years.

Anthony Powell

The Phrase Some Grew Up Hearing

"Go lay down. Mommy'll be back."

We heard it in the hallway.
We heard it in the courtroom.
We heard it in the living room after yet another fight with a man who was supposed to love us but only knew how to leave.

Sometimes she came back with food.
Sometimes she came back with bruises.
Sometimes she didn't come back at all.

Daddy was already gone. Long gone. Not just physically — but spiritually, emotionally, psychologically unavailable. For many Black children, "daddy" is a name, not a presence. A silhouette. A voicemail. A memory Mama won't speak on.

And what happens to a child — especially a boy — when his blueprint for manhood is built from silence? What happens to a girl when she only sees her mother break, never bloom?

In the U.S., over **64% of Black children** grow up in homes without their biological father present (U.S. Census Bureau, 2023). But don't let white conservatives weaponize that number without the whole truth. Black families were intentionally fractured — by slavery, by incarceration, by economic targeting. By systems designed to breed dependency and punish Black fatherhood.

The Welfare Myth and the Back-Door Truth

Let's address one of the most recycled narratives in our community — that *Black women kicked Black men out of the house for welfare.*

Yes, in the late 1960s and early 1970s, welfare policies like the "man-in-the-house" rules could penalize households if an able-bodied man was found living there. Yes, government inspectors sometimes came knocking, looking for men's clothes in the closet. But here's the thing — the **average welfare check in the 1970s was about $300 a month** (roughly $1,800 in today's money). That wasn't a fortune. It wasn't a magic ticket out of poverty.

The policy was real. But it was also a **perfect deflection** for some men who didn't want to be accountable.

Because if you really want to see your children — to raise them, guide them, love them — how does a $300 check stop you? How does any check stop you from being present? Plenty of men found a way — coming in through the back door, staying over at night, still raising their kids under the radar — because the bond was stronger than the policy.

WHY YOU SHOULDN'T EAT FROM SOME WHITE PEOPLE

The real dismantling of the Black home wasn't just a welfare rule — it was **systemic racism choking out economic opportunity**. Men shut out of stable jobs by hiring discrimination. Housing prices and rent gouged in Black neighborhoods, forcing families into overcrowded or unstable living situations. Factories closing. Unions blocking Black membership. Redlining keeping Black men from buying homes even when they had the income.

The government didn't just dangle a welfare check — they closed the doors to sustainable income and then blamed us for the fallout.

The Pipeline and the Partner

Some daddies didn't leave — they were locked away. The school-to-prison pipeline doesn't begin with a suspension slip. It begins with a little boy who doesn't know who to model. With a girl who's never seen a man love a woman gently.

And let's be honest — that pipeline starts before the baby is even born. It starts with **who you choose to lay with**. What you excuse. What you explain away as "potential."

Sometimes the red flags are waving like parade banners — but we call them "cultural quirks" or "just how men are." Then we're shocked when he ghosts after the baby shower, and your tears become the lullabies.

Understanding Mommy

Let's talk about Mommy. Not to shame her — to understand her. She's been holding down households with duct tape and divine grace. Working two jobs. Studying for her GED. Feeding children and fighting courts.

Black women are the most educated demographic in the U.S. right now (National Center for Education Statistics, 2020). But that education doesn't stop CPS from knocking. It doesn't pay the emotional debt of raising children and nursing wounds while being told she's "too bitter," "too strong," "too much."

Many never meant to raise their children alone. They were sold lies — romanticized struggle, charismatic narcissists, promises wrapped in manipulation. Some stayed longer than they should've. And now the house is cracked, but nobody wants to name the earthquake.

Survival vs. Intention

Most of us were raised in survival mode. Food on the table? That was love. A roof over your head? That was affection. No CPS at the door? That was good parenting.

But survival parenting doesn't raise whole children — it raises functioning adults with hidden grief. We didn't learn emotional regulation — we learned suppression. We didn't learn communication — we learned avoidance.

When Daddy left — physically or spiritually — the home didn't just lose structure. It lost balance.

What We Inherited

For boys: Watching Mama do everything either turns you into a man who looks for women to save you or a man who resents women with power. Without a father's love and structure, masculinity becomes performance — dominance over devotion.

For girls: Growing up seeing Mama cry into her pillow teaches you that love is earned through endurance. That struggle is a requirement for Black love to feel "real." That a baby can anchor a man.

WHY YOU SHOULDN'T EAT FROM SOME WHITE PEOPLE

It's not love — it's trauma bonding.

You're Not Fine, You're Functioning

"Ain't never had no daddy, and I turned out fine." No — you turned out functioning. Fine people don't flinch at love or self-sabotage healthy relationships. Fine people don't confuse chaos with chemistry.

Fatherlessness distorts identity. Without that affirmation, structure, and guidance, children piece themselves together from scraps — sometimes dangerous ones.

Familiar Doesn't Mean Healthy

When abandonment is your first form of love, you start choosing what feels familiar, not what's healthy. You chase chaos because calm feels foreign. You accept inconsistency because you learned to explain away Daddy's absence.

We've got to stop spiritualizing inconsistency. Stop calling abandonment "a test from God" when it's really a test of your boundaries.

Facts & Forward

- **64%** of Black children live in single-parent homes, most often with their mother (U.S. Census Bureau, 2023).
- Black fathers are more likely to live apart from their children than white or Latino fathers, but among those who are present, they are **the most involved fathers in America** (CDC, 2013).
- Children in single-parent homes are at greater statistical risk for school dropout, poverty, incarceration, and behavioral issues.

Parenting doesn't start when the baby is born — it starts with partner choice. If you co-parent with someone who doesn't love themselves, you're co-parenting trauma.

Rebuilding the Village

We need a real village again. Not the gossip kind — the kind that catches you when you fall. That picks up the kids without making you feel like a burden.

Because what's happening isn't just neglect — it's warfare. And our children are the casualties.

Daddy being gone was never supposed to be the norm. Mommy shouldn't have to keep coming back from brokenness to keep the house standing.

The Only Way Forward

It's not about blaming Daddy anymore. It's about accountability from *everyone*.
Men — stop hiding behind the welfare myth when you just didn't want the weight of fatherhood.
Women — stop romanticizing struggle and calling it strength.

Our children deserve presence, not just proximity.
And the revolution in Black family life starts with this: **We stay. We show up. We heal before we hand our pain to the next generation.**

Next Steps

- Stop having babies with people who can't commit to you or themselves. If they won't commit to marriage, why assume they'll commit to parenthood?
- Be honest before intimacy. Ask yourself: Do I want this person tied to my child forever?

- Watch how someone treats the kids they already have. That's your blueprint.
- Create routines. Eat together. Talk together. Read together. Build stability into your child's nervous system.
- Engage with your kids. Even if they talk your ears off, they need your ears. It's not just cute. It's critical.
- Model the kind of partner you want your child to become or attract. Ask: Would I want my son or daughter with someone like me?

Legacy is not what you leave in your will. It's what you model in your living. So parent like a healthy village is watching. Parent like your grandchild's healing depends on it. Because it does.

Daddy and mommy are back—with wisdom, with wounds, and with a new way. And this time, we're raising children who know they are loved. Because love didn't leave—it led.

🪶 Reflection & Growth

What emotions did this page stir in you?

_____

_____

_____

_____

How have you seen this play out in your family or community?

_____

_____

_____

_____

What's one action you can take to interrupt that cycle?

_____

_____

_____

_____

CHAPTER FOURTEEN
YOUR CHILD CAN'T READ BECAUSE OF YOU

> The question is not whether we can afford to invest in every child; it is whether we can afford not to.
> **Marian Wright Edelman**

The Power of Knowledge

One of the longest-standing truths known to humanity is this: without knowledge, you perish — not just mentally, but economically, socially, spiritually, and generationally. From our tribal African ancestors to the children being funneled through America's underperforming school systems today, the through-line is simple: **education is liberation.** And the lack of it is a cage, whether made of chains or cheap digital distractions.

A Present-Day Picture

Picture this: A 9-year-old Black boy sits at his desk, lips moving but no sound coming out. He's trying to read a passage his classmates finished a minute ago. His head drops. The teacher moves on.

Now picture another child — same age, same school — who eagerly raises her hand because she's read the book at home with her mother three times already. She knows the story, the words, and the confidence of being prepared.

The difference isn't always intelligence. Sometimes it's exposure. Sometimes it's environment. Sometimes it's whether they've *seen* reading modeled in their own home.

Ancient African Education

Before our ancestors were chained and forced onto ships, they were already educated. They knew agriculture, engineering, astronomy, metallurgy, textile making, herbal medicine, trade systems, and governance. These skills weren't random — they were taught, practiced, and preserved through communal knowledge and cultural rituals. In many African societies, children were trained in trades, languages, philosophy, and spiritual systems from a young age. Education was not separated from identity — **it was identity**. Knowing your language, your story, your gifts — that was tradition and survival.

Knowledge as a Threat to Oppression

When Europeans colonized and enslaved, they knew: if you want to own a people, erase their access to knowledge. That's why enslaved Africans were legally forbidden to learn to read or write. That's why pages of the Bible were ripped out. That's why oral stories were severed.

And that's why, centuries later, Black Americans still feel the aftershocks — questioning their value, struggling in school systems designed for someone else, and watching generations drown in digital media while their academic skills decline.

The Slave Bible and Spiritual Erasure

During slavery, the Bible was often the only book allowed in Black quarters — but even that was censored. Slave owners used something called the "Slave Bible," which removed nearly 90% of the Old Testament and half of the New. Gone were stories of liberation, revolution, and divine justice. Left behind were messages about obedience and servitude.

Even spiritual learning was manipulated. Yet the Black church became one of the first spaces where literacy and self-education were reclaimed — where the Bible became both a tool of faith and a weapon of freedom.

Modern Literacy Crisis

According to the National Center for Education Statistics, **only 18% of Black 4th graders are proficient in reading.** One in four Black students will drop out of high school, often due to academic deficits. By third grade, literacy levels are used to project future prison populations.

That's not coincidence — that's a pipeline. And the school-to-prison pipeline is paved with unread books, unchallenged curriculums, and unchecked environments at home.

The Role of Parents in the Literacy Gap

If you want your child to read better, you can't leave it all to the school. Your child needs to see you reading — books, articles, instructions, anything. When a child watches a parent engage with written words, they learn that reading is valuable, normal, and even enjoyable.

And your presence in their school matters. When a child sees their parent show up to volunteer, read to the class, or meet with teachers, it tells them: *Education matters to my family.* Research shows children whose parents are active in their school environment are more likely to have better attendance, higher reading scores, and fewer behavioral issues.

Black Male Teachers Matter

Representation matters. Studies show that Black students — especially Black boys — are more likely to graduate high school if they have even **one Black teacher** in elementary school. For Black boys from low-income households, having a Black male teacher in the early years can cut dropout rates nearly in half.

A Black male teacher can model literacy, leadership, and learning in ways that counter stereotypes. But until we have more of them, fathers, uncles, and community men can step into that gap by reading to children, speaking at schools, or simply being seen valuing education.

Economic Power Through Learning

Education opens doors. People with a high school diploma earn, on average, $9,000 more annually than those without one. Trade skills can bring $45,000 to $80,000 per year. Associate and bachelor's degree holders earn between $50,000 and $75,000 on average — more with postgraduate work.

But money isn't the only currency education gives you — it's also confidence. It lets you read a lease before you sign it, decode a health diagnosis, negotiate a salary, or spot a scam.

Trade Skills Require Education

Not everybody's meant for college — but *everybody* is meant to learn. Welders, mechanics, barbers, beauticians, plumbers — every one of those fields requires reading, comprehension, and precision. You can't master the tools of your trade if you can't understand the language they come with.

The Value of the Arts

Children in music, drama, dance, or visual arts programs score higher in overall academic performance. Art teaches discipline, memory, collaboration, and creativity — all transferable to reading and problem-solving. Historically, the Black community has excelled in the arts — gospel, jazz, hip-hop, quilting, murals — but when arts are stripped from our schools, especially underfunded ones, we lose both skill and spirit.

Cultural Education and Identity

Many ethnic groups intentionally link education to cultural pride. Jewish, Asian, and Latino families build identity alongside academics. Too often, Black children are handed a curriculum that starts with slavery, erasing millennia of African achievement.

That's why your home must teach what schools often won't — about Mali, Kemet, Nubia, Ethiopia — so your child's sense of self doesn't start with chains.

The Educational Revolution Starts at Home

Get a library card. Read with your child every day. Fifteen minutes a day can change a life. Let them read to you. Let them see you reading. Fill your home with books that look like them, sound like them, and teach them their own history.

Be present at their school — even once a month. Support their teachers. Demand better curricula. Protect the arts. And most of all, make education a family value, not just a school requirement.

This is a quiet revolution. And if we don't lead it, somebody else will — and it won't be for our freedom.

Next Steps:
• Get a library card and make visiting the library a family tradition.
• Read and study together. Choose a family book each month that reflects your heritage and values.

- Set learning goals in your household that are not tied to school grades but to life skills—like writing a letter, learning budgeting, or researching ancestry.
- Support your child in learning a trade, instrument, or cultural tradition as much as you support sports or social media access.
- Have weekly check-ins about what everyone is learning—not just in school, but in life.
- Partner with another family to build a small educational pod—reading group, STEM club, cultural film night.
- Reclaim storytelling. Share family stories. Record elders talking about their lives. Turn your home into a living archive.
- Attend school board meetings. Be present. Let your voice shape the curriculum and culture of your child's school.
- Remove shame from struggle. If your child is behind, don't ignore it—support them with grace, structure, and expectation.
- Make education visible. Let your children see you learning—reading, researching, asking questions, and growing.
- Build a legacy of learning that doesn't depend on the system but thrives in spite of it.

Why This Matters

Because in this world, education is armor. It's a map. It's a sword. And it's a signal to the world that you will not be silenced, sold, or stopped. So if you're wondering why your child can't excel academically, ask yourself if you've handed them anything worth learning. Or better yet—if you're learning yourself.

WHY YOU SHOULDN'T EAT FROM SOME WHITE PEOPLE

🪶 Reflection & Growth

What excuses came to mind while reading this?

_____

_____

_____

_____

If you removed the excuses, what would be possible?

_____

_____

_____

_____

What small but bold step can you take toward that possibility?

_____

_____

_____

_____

CHAPTER FIFTEEN
BLACK MEN LEFT BLACK MEN BEHIND

"Am I my brother's keeper?"
Nino Brown

"A legacy with no community is just a lonely monument."

Too many Black men make it out and close the door behind them. Success becomes a solo mission—get the degree, the job, the house, the wife, the peace. But what about the block you left behind? The boys who watched you grow up from the porch, hoping your win meant maybe they could win too? This isn't just a failure of economics—it's a failure of collective purpose.

Black vagina freed us from bondage, but the Black phallus often keeps us in bondage.

The womb of the Black woman carried us through the transatlantic slave trade, labored on plantations, nursed white babies, and birthed generations of resistance. That same womb was fetishized by white men, leading to a twisted kind of selective "mercy"—some women freed, some given land, some children secretly educated. It was a distorted lens of desire and possession, not justice, but it occasionally granted survival.

Meanwhile, Black phallacy—the illusion that white proximity equals power—has had the opposite effect. From Jack Johnson to modern athletes and executives, many Black men have gambled freedom, money, and legacy chasing white acceptance through white women, white institutions, and whitewashed identities. They marry out, move their money out, and build families that often sever roots. White patriarchal power lets them visit the house but never own it.

According to the Pew Research Center (2022), nearly 24% of Black men in America marry outside their race—the highest rate among any ethnic male group. Their children are twice as likely to marry white partners, often erasing African lineage in just two or three generations. Cultural memory fades, ancestral pride disappears, and what began as "Black excellence" becomes barely recognizable as Black at all.

This is not about hate—it's about history, about how sexual politics have been weaponized to divide us, and about naming the ways we've confused assimilation for advancement while losing community in the process.

Brotherlessness Is the New Epidemic

It's not just fatherlessness that's killing us—it's brotherlessness. We are short on elders, uncles, accountability, and safe spaces for men to bleed, build, and be better. That's no accident.

Slavery auctioned off our men, separated them from children, and criminalized their presence. Black men were stripped of authority and the role of household head. Keep a people disorganized, disconnected, and competing, and they will self-destruct.

Fast forward to the 1970s and '80s—mass incarceration became the new genocide. Black men are still locked up at five times the rate of white men. According to the Sentencing Project (2023), over one in three Black boys born today can expect to go to prison if nothing changes. The school-to-prison pipeline outpaced trade schools, and too few elders stood on the sidewalk saying, "Come home, youngblood. I see you."

WHY YOU SHOULDN'T EAT FROM SOME WHITE PEOPLE

Even those who find success often keep their distance. Black men in boardrooms won't hire brothers with records. Athletes post sneakers but not scholarships. Rappers drop mixtapes but not ladders. Some even deny racism exists. The truth? Too many don't trust each other enough to share the code.

Success Without Healing Is Just High-Functioning Brokenness

Many "successful" Black men still operate in survival mode—wealth without wellness, status without safety, keys they don't share. Pain gets replaced with performance, presence with appearance. They inspire envy, not growth.

Hyper-individualism tells us legacy is about who dies with the most money. White men don't think that way—they pass down playbooks, internships, and coaching. We hand down silence and vague warnings: "Don't get locked up. Don't knock her up. Don't mess it up."

We have boys trying to be men with no blueprint—just vibes, YouTube, and rap lyrics.

The Performance of Masculinity Is Killing Us

We were taught to perform strength, not process pain. So we become emotionally illiterate, parenting from trauma, leading from fear, loving from insecurity.

Black adults are 20% more likely to experience serious mental health problems than the general population, yet Black men are the least likely to seek therapy. Suicide among Black men has risen 23% in the last decade. We've been trained to suffer in silence—drink through it, fight through it, disappear when crumbling.

Masculinity is presence, not performance. It's measured by the lives you protect, the boys you counsel, the tears you make safe, the families you stand in the gap for. You don't have to be fully healed to help—you just have to show up.

Black Men Are Not Disposable—They're Foundational

Black men are essential to the healing and structure of neighborhoods, families, and the economy. Children with actively engaged fathers are 60% less likely to be suspended, 75% less likely to experience teen pregnancy, and twice as likely to attend college.

Systemic forces have worked overtime to remove Black men from households, but when present, Black fathers are more involved in daily caregiving than any other group of fathers in the U.S.

The question is not whether Black men are good enough—it's what changes when they stop being forced to do it alone.

Economic Power Lies in Brotherhood

Black spending power reached $1.3 trillion in 2019, yet the Black dollar circulates in our communities for less than six hours. Internal disconnection adds to systemic theft.

Too many still chase individual wealth over collective wealth. We build portfolios, not playgrounds; luxury brands, not legacy structures. Poverty won't be fixed without repairing the disconnection between Black men and communal purpose.

The Cost of Disengaged Masculinity

When Black men are absent, gangs, clout chasers, and toxic influencers fill the vacuum. Girls grow up unprotected, streets become classrooms, and trauma becomes a rite of passage.

Communities with low male presence see higher poverty, lower educational attainment, more crime, and reduced social mobility.

But when Black men engage, neighborhoods stabilize, children thrive, businesses grow, and safety improves.

Stop Glorifying Survival—Start Uplifting Stability

We clap louder for the man who survived hell than for the one who avoided it. We repost mugshots, not mentorship. We must celebrate the men who stayed, raised their kids, worked honest jobs, and said "no" to the streets.

Success is not just escape—it's refusing to replicate struggle in the next generation.

We Can't Heal What We Keep Hiding

Vulnerability has been framed as weakness, so we bury our pain until it shows up as violence, addiction, or collapse. Many live in functional pain—present in body, absent in spirit.

Silent suffering isn't noble—it's deadly. Men who've endured abuse, loss, and trauma often have nowhere safe to say, "I'm hurting." So they ghost their families, self-medicate, or disappear into isolation.

What if instead of "man up," we said, "Let me walk with you"?

Presence Is the Real Protection

Being present doesn't require perfection—just consistency. Presence stabilizes the next generation, models emotional regulation, and teaches love, process, and recovery.

And it's not just about the nuclear family—when Black men engage as teachers, coaches, business owners, and OGs, crime drops, graduation rates rise, and the cultural tone shifts.

Legacy Isn't What You Leave—It's Who You Lift

Legacy is not how many cars you bought or followers you gained—it's who you protected, mentored, and lifted. Every healed man plants seeds of protection, stability, and wealth for generations.

You don't need a platform to be powerful or perfection to be purposeful—you just need to show up on purpose.

You Are the Blueprint, Not the Exception

There's a boy watching how you move—how you handle women, money, stress, and disrespect. You are not just a story—you are a system.

Brotherhood is not optional—it's oxygen. Be the uncle who checks in, the coach who shows up, the mentor who listens, the OG who redirects. Mentorship is a posture, not a title.

Tools for Brotherhood

1. **If you got out, go back.** Not to stay—but to sow. Speak at the school you went to. Sponsor a kid from your neighborhood. Show your face where you once hid your pain.
2. **Create a circle, not a following.** Start a text thread. A breakfast meetup. A check-in call. Make brotherhood a lifestyle, not a once-a-year event.
3. **Go to therapy—and tell another man you did.** Normalize healing. Let's stop treating therapy like it's weakness. It's a weapon. Use it.

4. **Protect our boys from early death—spiritual or literal.** Be the reason a young man chooses school over the streets. Peace over proving himself. Living over surviving.
5. **Stop clapping for men who abandon—and start affirming those who stay.** Celebrate healthy commitment. Assist ones who want to leave a bad situation. Applaud growth. Honor responsibility.

Final Word: You Are the Standard

Black men, you are not missing—you are needed.

Not just in protest. Not just in profit. In *presence*. In proximity. In participation. If we don't lead our boys and girls, the world will. If we don't mentor each other, the media will raise us. If we don't build a brotherhood, we will bury another one.

And I don't know about you—but I'm tired of going to funerals for men who died alone in rooms full of applause.

Let's change the story. Let's bring our brothers back.

Reflection & Growth

What generational pattern do you see reflected here?

_____

_____

_____

_____

How has it touched your own story?

_____

_____

_____

_____

What step can you take to be the one who breaks it?

_____

_____

_____

_____

CHAPTER SIXTEEN
IN THE LA LA LAND OF US NEVER INTEGRATING

"Integration didn't liberate us — it diluted us."

The Great Illusion of Togetherness

We thought we were getting free.
When the cameras flashed and Black children walked, heads high, into all-white schools guarded by soldiers, the world called it a triumph. A victory for equality. The American Dream folding its arms around all its citizens at last.

But in hindsight, we weren't walking into freedom — we were walking into a fantasy. And not the kind that heals. The kind that hypnotizes.

Integration was marketed as a cure to racism. But what it really was, was a performance. A pacifier for a system that never repented, never paid reparations, and never intended to love us.

We bought into the lie that being allowed into their spaces would make us equal. That we'd be treated better if we wore the same clothes, spoke the same way, walked the same hallways. But assimilation is not liberation. It's camouflage.

La La Land whispered that proximity to whiteness meant progress. And some of us believed it. We believed that if we could just attend their schools, live in their neighborhoods, marry into their families, we'd be safe. Respected. Fed.

But La La Land was never real. It was a studio lot dressed up like justice. They didn't integrate to love us. They integrated to manage us. And in the process, we lost the most important thing we had: each other.

What We Traded for Their Tables

We had thriving communities. We had rhythm, enterprise, pride. We had barbers who knew our granddaddy's hairline, doctors who didn't dismiss our pain, and teachers who saw our children as more than trouble. We had what we needed — though not always what we wanted. But what we had was ours.

In the pursuit of validation, we traded away ecosystems that had sustained us through the worst of American terror. Communities like Greenwood in Tulsa, Oklahoma — Black Wall Street — weren't just financial success stories, they were blueprints for what Black autonomy looked like when left to bloom.

We had our own banks, hospitals, insurance firms, movie theaters, grocery stores. The dollar circulated within the Black community up to 100 times before it left. Now? Less than once.

And the same happened with our schools. Before Brown v. Board of Education in 1954, Black children were taught by Black teachers who loved them, prayed for them, and sometimes taught in buildings held together with duct tape and hope.

Here's what's rarely discussed: those Black educators were, on average, more qualified and better trained than many of their white counterparts — because they had to be. And yet, after integration, they were fired en masse. Not for lack of skill — but because white school boards didn't want Black adults in authority over white children.

We didn't just lose Black schools. We lost a generation of Black intellectual mentorship, accountability, and academic pride.

The Negro Leagues and the Price of Proximity

One of the clearest examples of integration-as-erasure was the Negro Baseball League.

It wasn't just a place for athletes — it was an economic powerhouse. It employed Black ticket vendors, ushers, concession workers, sportswriters, and hotel owners. It created a full economy around Black talent that circulated money, culture, and pride within the community.

When Jackie Robinson broke the color line in 1947, and other players followed him into Major League Baseball, it wasn't just a win — it was a warning. Black players were cherry-picked for white stadiums, but the Negro League was not preserved.

It collapsed under the weight of our excitement to be "included." Instead of integrating the leagues, they integrated the players. Our institutions were never merged — they were mined. Our value was extracted. Our legacy was left to rot.

The Psychology of Proximity

What integration did to us psychologically, we still haven't fully unpacked.

Nobody was calling it what it was at the time: a collective trauma response. A need to be seen as "just as good" in a world that told us we were three-fifths. So, many Black folks didn't just want access — they wanted validation.

They took their dollars out of Black neighborhoods and gave them to white diners, white shops, and white businesses, not because those places treated them better, but because spending there made them feel equal. There's a scene in *Lovecraft Country* where Montrose says, 'They'll take our money because it's just as good as anyone else's.'

We didn't see that in chasing inclusion, we were evacuating our own ecosystems.

The Cost of What Was Taken — Land, Labor, and Legacy

We didn't just give things up. They were stolen.

According to a 2022 report by the Center for American Progress, Black farmers have lost more than 90% of their farmland since 1910 — over 12 million acres, primarily due to racist lending practices, intimidation, legal loopholes, and systemic discrimination by the USDA. That land today would be worth over **$326 billion**. That's not just dirt — that's intergenerational wealth, vanished."

Even before that theft of acreage, we were betrayed. After the Civil War, the promise of *"40 acres and a mule"* was meant to be the seedbed of Black freedom — a tangible start to generational stability. Instead, Andrew Johnson reversed the order, handing those parcels right back to former Confederate planters. Fires destroyed deeds. Banks shut us out of loans. Courts and sheriffs pushed through fake foreclosure claims. Land that could have been the bedrock for schools, farms, small businesses — wealth Black families could pass down — was stolen before it could bloom. Today, U.S. cropland is worth about **$5,830 per acre**. Imagine if even half a million acres had remained in Black hands — we would be talking about **trillions** in legacy wealth, community infrastructure, and economic independence. Instead, those acres became the foundation of someone else's empire — and another generation's bargain for acceptance.

WHY YOU SHOULDN'T EAT FROM SOME WHITE PEOPLE

Land isn't just about farming — it's leverage. It's collateral for loans, a foundation for housing and businesses, a power you can pass down.

And then there's our intellectual property. Garrett Morgan created the traffic light and gas mask. Dr. Shirley Jackson helped develop caller ID. Frederick McKinley Jones developed refrigeration systems used in trucks — key to the modern cold food supply chain.

Yet patents were often stolen or re-registered by white intermediaries. Music, fashion, slang, style — all exported without compensation. Our culture became their currency.

When the wealth generated by Black innovation is funneled into white institutions, we don't just lose money — we lose power.

Strategic Separation — Not Segregation

We don't need to go back to segregation. But we do need **strategic separation** — building our own systems without waiting for theirs to make room.

We need Black banks that underwrite our hustlers, Black schools that teach our real history, Black mental health professionals who understand ancestral trauma.

Ecosystems are more than markets — they're communities, economies, and cultures that feed each other. When one wins, all win. That's what we had before integration — and that's what we must now choose to reclaim.

Wake Up, Rebuild, Return

We have ancestors who built with less and did more. Who started schools under trees and banks in barbershops.

We don't need a handout. We need a handoff — from one generation of Black brilliance to the next.

La La Land is closed. It's time for us to be the architects. Not in someone else's name — but in the name of every ancestor who refused to die with their head bowed.

Next Steps and Challenges — Reclaiming Our Table

You don't need to burn bridges—just start building new roads. Integration may have given us access, but it never gave us agency. These next steps are about reclaiming what we gave away: our systems, our safety nets, our standards.

1. Build Intentional Circles

Stop waiting for "the culture" to support you. Start with five people and build from there. Form investment circles, business partnerships, and mutual aid groups with people who share your values. You don't need a million followers—just a movement of commitment.

2. Spend with Strategy

Support Black-owned banks, service providers, and platforms. Don't just shop Black—*scale Black*. Refer them. Review them. Invest in them. Make it a habit, not a hashtag.

3. Re-Educate Ourselves and Our Children

Teach what the schools won't. African history, land ownership, economic survival, spiritual protection, and media literacy. Make your dinner table, your living room, your group chats—*the classroom*.

4. Prioritize Land and Legacy

Buy the land, even if it's modest. Establish family trusts. Put elders on your business accounts and youth in your business plans. Make decisions that your grandchildren will benefit from, not just your followers.

5. Control the Narrative

Start the podcast. Write the book. Record the family stories. Archive your grandmother's recipes and your uncle's wisdom. Don't wait for permission to preserve your legacy. Media is memory—and we must own ours.

Your Challenge:
Don't mourn integration. *Learn from it.*
Don't chase the old table. *Flip it.*
Build a new one. Fill it with people who remember what we lost—
and are ready to multiply what we still have.

🐦 Reflection & Growth

What excuses came to mind while reading this?

_____

_____

_____

_____

If you removed the excuses, what would be possible?

_____

_____

_____

_____

What small but bold step can you take toward that possibility?

_____

_____

_____

_____

CHAPTER SEVENTEEN
THE GOVERNMENT DOESN'T CARE BECAUSE YOU DON'T

Si Vis Pacem, Para Bellum".
("If you want peace, prepare for war")
- **Flavius Vegetius Renatus. Roman Military strategist. c. 390. A.**

Where Government Really Began

Governments didn't start in Washington, D.C. They started in Africa—in kingdoms that predate the pyramids. Ethiopia had emperors before England had a name. Nubia had queens who commanded armies and managed economies. These weren't scattered huts; they were organized, wealthy, powerful civilizations.

Africa is the birthplace of governance, trade, law, and diplomacy. But even in those days, the root of governance was control—through fear, through faith, through food. Before there was a ballot box, there was the fear of divine punishment or the shame of dishonoring your ancestors. Religion was the earliest government—systemic, structured, and binding. People obeyed because their soul was on the line.

That grip hasn't gone away. It just swapped sacred scrolls for constitutions and pulpits for podiums. And here in America, "democracy" has always been complicated for us. Black people were brought here to *build* a government we were never meant to *participate* in. Counted as three-fifths of a person. Beaten, taxed, and terrorized for trying to vote. Centuries of being told, "You don't belong here."

Our disengagement from politics isn't laziness—it's survival fatigue. But the irony? The people who built this nation's foundation still have the power to reshape it. If we remember who we were before oppression, we'd stop acting like change is impossible. Our ancestors understood power. Now it's on us to reclaim it.

Like Pericles said—and Ella Baker, Fannie Lou Hamer, and Stacey Abrams lived—"You may not be interested in politics, but politics is interested in you."

Bought and Paid For: Who Really Leads

In America, leaders don't rise because of integrity. They rise because they're bankrolled. This country runs on lobbyist money, campaign donations, and political favors. The person with the fattest war chest usually wins—not the one with the strongest plan for the people.

W.E.B. Du Bois warned in *The Souls of Black Folk*: "The ruling of men is based not on justice, but on the control of property." Nothing's changed. Billionaires still have the lawmakers' ear while working-class voices get drowned out.

In 2024 alone, over **$20 billion** was poured into federal, state, and local elections. And the top fundraisers won **90%** of the time. Meanwhile, we're told politics is boring. That it doesn't matter. That we should chase the bag instead of the ballot. But here's the truth—**your bag is being taxed, legislated, and regulated by people you didn't even bother to vote for.**

WHY YOU SHOULDN'T EAT FROM SOME WHITE PEOPLE

Black America spends **$1.6 trillion** annually. That's global economic force money. But without political leverage, that spending power never turns into policy power.

And this is where we fail ourselves—when we elect people and then walk away. We put them in office, then never check back in. If someone is asking for your vote, you should already have their cell number, email, or public meeting schedule saved. **If they're not meeting your needs, you should be in their inbox, at their town halls, and on their public record demanding answers.** We can't just elect people who say the right things—we have to elect people who *do* the right things and then make sure they keep doing them.

Representatives Out of Touch
Most elected officials—especially white politicians—have never worked a day outside of politics. They've been interns, clerks, networked up in college, and stayed within the bubble ever since. In fact, working-class Americans make up nearly **half the population**, yet they hold only **about 2%** of Congressional seats That means the folks electing policy often haven't lived the struggles that policy should address.
And when officials don't live in or around lower-income communities, how can they truly know what those neighborhoods need? Their decisions are made in suites, not on streets with potholes and closed schools.
That's why, when we elect people, we must **stay connected**—get their district phone, go to their meetings, email them when our streets, youth programs, or healthcare access is getting shortchanged. Let them know we're watching, and that our lives depend on it.

Reaganomics and Economic Sabotage

Ronald Reagan didn't just cut taxes—he cut the working class off at the knees. He sold America a lie that still lives today: that helping the rich would "trickle down" to everyone else. Forty years later, we're still standing under that faucet, dry. The only thing that trickles down is poverty.

Reaganomics gutted social programs like housing assistance, job training, and education grants while opening the floodgates for corporate greed. His "War on Drugs" wasn't about safety—it was about criminalizing poverty and Blackness.

From 2000 to 2007, the U.S. debt ceiling jumped from **$4.5 trillion** to **$11.6 trillion**, mostly to fund wars and corporate subsidies. Social Security's trust fund? Raided for **$2.5 trillion**. Then they claimed there wasn't enough money for healthcare, schools, or student debt relief.

The result? The median white family now holds over **eight times** the wealth of the median Black family—a gap that's barely moved in 50 years. That's not mismanagement. That's intentional.

Redirecting the Blame

It's easy to say, "Our people just don't care," but look closer. Are your schools underfunded? Roads crumbling? Grocery stores replaced by liquor stores? That's not your neighbor's laziness—that's a political decision.

In Chicago, a child born in the South Side has a **30-year shorter life expectancy** than one born just nine miles away in Lincoln Park. That's policy. That's zoning. That's budget priorities.

When we see decay, crime, and neglect, we need to ask: **Who benefits from this staying broken?** And then we need to confront *them*, not each other.

The Lie of Educational Equality

WHY YOU SHOULDN'T EAT FROM SOME WHITE PEOPLE

Integration gave us access—but not equality. Our kids were bused into schools that didn't want them, handed outdated books, and punished harder than white students for the same behaviors. Malcolm X said, "Only a fool would let his enemy educate his children." And yet, we've trusted a system built without us in mind.

Today, the erasure is slicker. AP African American Studies is blocked in some states. Books banned. Curriculums sanitized. Black students are **four times** more likely to be suspended, **three times** less likely to be in gifted programs, and more likely to attend schools without art, music, or mental health services.

This is why *local* elections matter. School boards control curriculums. County commissioners control school funding. If we don't show up there, we forfeit our children's future before they ever graduate.

Healthcare Isn't Healing Us

Black women are **three times** more likely to die during childbirth. Black men are less likely to be prescribed pain medication for the same ailments as white men. Hospitals close in poor neighborhoods not by accident, but by policy.

The Tuskegee experiment wasn't a one-off—it was a blueprint. Today's healthcare deserts, delayed diagnoses, and lack of cultural competence are all part of the same pattern: profit over people.

Voting for local and state leaders directly affects whether Medicaid expands, where clinics get built, and which communities receive preventive care. Healthcare is political—always has been.

You Are the First Line of Defense

Whether you rent or own, your block is your responsibility. Pride in community starts with small actions: picking up trash, speaking to neighbors, helping elders, obeying speed limits where kids play.

But it also means *showing up*—to zoning meetings, budget hearings, and city council sessions. Gentrification doesn't just "happen"—it's planned, approved, and signed off in rooms we often don't enter.

If you can't go in person, email. Call. Make your name known to the people making decisions about your street.

We Are Not Powerless

We're not powerless—we're unorganized. Every time we save a neighbor's home, run a grassroots campaign, or shut down injustice, we prove our capacity. But hashtags aren't enough. Change comes from habits: voting, mentoring, questioning, showing up.

Our ancestors bled for the ballot. Treat it like the sacred tool it is. Imagine if we tracked our elected officials like we do celebrity drama. Imagine if voting day had Black Friday energy.

The legacy we leave can't just be about surviving. It has to be about *strategically winning*.

The Call

If we want the government to care, we have to make them. That means electing people who have our interests at heart—and not just believing them because they smile in a Black church during campaign season. It means *watching them* after the election. Showing up at their meetings. Emailing when our needs aren't met. Holding receipts.

WHY YOU SHOULDN'T EAT FROM SOME WHITE PEOPLE

Show up. Speak up. Stay consistent. The system belongs to the people who use it. And right now? Too many of us are leaving it on the table.

We are the leaders we've been waiting for. But we're still waiting on ourselves.

Here's what you can do this week—no excuses:

- **Find out when your next local election is.** Put it in your phone and set a reminder.
- **Register to vote.** Make sure your address is current. Help someone else do the same.
- **Look up your city councilperson.** Send one email about something that needs fixing in your community.
- **Walk your block.** Clean up trash. Say hello to your neighbors. Ask someone how they're doing.
- **Talk to your kids about leadership.** Teach them that their voice matters now—not just when they grow up.
- **Post something about civic engagement.** Whether it's a meeting, a voting date, or a resource—share it.
- **Ask your church, mosque, barbershop, or hair salon to put up a voter info board.** These are our hubs—use them.

And then do it again next week. And the week after that.

Because consistency builds power. Because engagement builds protection. Because visibility builds respect.

You don't have to change the world overnight. Just change your corner of it. Because when one block lights up, the whole street sees it.

We are not invisible. We are not voiceless. We are not powerless. We are the storm. And it's time they heard us coming.

🎤 Reflection & Growth

Who in your life needs to hear this?

_____

_____

_____

_____

How will you bring it to them?

_____

_____

_____

_____

What action will you model so they see it lived, not just spoken?

_____

_____

_____

_____

CHAPTER EIGHTEEN
STOP INVESTING IN DEPRECIABLE PEOPLE

You're either part of the solution or part of the problem.
(Leroy) Eldridge Cleaver

The Broken Car Metaphor

Some of us keep pouring time, energy, and money into people who depreciate our value—not add to it. Imagine putting all your savings into a broken down car that hasn't moved in years. You repaint it, replace the tires, even install new speakers. But the engine won't start. You don't need more love for that car—you need more wisdom. It's not going anywhere, and neither are you if you stay attached.

That's what it's like when we invest in people who have no intention of growing. Who won't fix what's broken inside of them. Who treat our sacrifice like scraps. And too often, we do it in the name of loyalty, family, love, or history. We mistake guilt for obligation, and emotional debt for destiny.

We grew up watching our mothers carry too much, watching uncles squander support, watching siblings get chance after chance while the responsible child got silence and stress. It wasn't called enabling back then—it was just called love. But the result is the same: exhaustion with no reward, generational patterns with no growth, and cycles of trauma that block wealth, health, and wholeness.

We keep repairing what God didn't even assign us to fix. We call it compassion, but it's codependency dressed in Sunday clothes. Some of us are afraid to stop because we think if we're not saving people, we're not worthy ourselves. But you were never meant to be their Jesus—you were meant to be a steward of peace, purpose, and power.

Guilt-Based Loyalty

We've been conditioned to believe that setting boundaries makes us selfish. That cutting off unhealthy relatives is wrong. That we owe old friends our energy because they "knew us when." But we don't owe anyone our peace. We don't owe access to people who constantly prove they can't be trusted with it.

Many of us grew up in households where words like narcissist, enabler, or boundaries weren't even in our vocabulary. We didn't have the terms, but we lived the behavior. We were taught that sacrifice without limits was love—and that helping people meant losing yourself in the process.

We carry guilt because we believe saying "no" is a rejection of our roots. But it's the opposite: knowing where you come from should make you more committed to breaking the cycle.

Guilt-based loyalty will bankrupt you—financially, spiritually, and emotionally. You'll lose sleep while they repeat the same patterns, because your effort becomes their excuse to avoid responsibility. Sometimes letting them fall is the only way they'll rise.

Bail Money vs. College Money – Where Are We Really Investing?

WHY YOU SHOULDN'T EAT FROM SOME WHITE PEOPLE

Let's keep it real with the numbers. The Prison Policy Initiative reports that Americans spend **$14 billion every year** just to post bail — and because Black Americans are disproportionately arrested, we carry a huge chunk of that load. Meanwhile, the U.S. Department of Education found that in the same year, **less than $6 billion in scholarships** went to Black students.

So, as a community, we're literally spending **over twice as much** getting folks out of jail as we are getting our young people into college. Now, I'm not saying don't help your people, but imagine what would shift if even half that bail money went into tuition, trade school, or seed money for businesses. Instead of getting someone out of a cell, you'd be setting them up for a seat at the table.

The Ripple Effect of Repeat Bailouts

A 2019 Harvard study on incarceration costs found that families in Black communities spend **an average of $13,607 per year** supporting an incarcerated loved one through bail, commissary, phone calls, and legal fees. Multiply that by just ten households on your block, and that's **$136,070 bleeding out of the neighborhood every year** — money that could've been used for down payments, starting businesses, or paying off debt.

Now ask yourself: How many of those same people got a college savings account for their child? How many have life insurance? How many have even $500 in emergency savings? We can't cry "systemic oppression" and keep doing systemic sabotage to ourselves.

The Hidden Cost of Emotional Support

It's not just the money that drains you — it's the mental and emotional labor. The American Psychological Association found that **Black adults report higher levels of emotional support-giving than any other racial group**, often to multiple family members at once. That sounds noble, but it comes at a cost:

Black caregivers are **63% more likely** to experience symptoms of anxiety and depression compared to non-caregivers.

A 2022 CDC report linked chronic emotional stress to **higher rates of hypertension, sleep disorders, and even weakened immune systems**. So when you're constantly the one answering late-night calls, mediating drama, or carrying someone else's crisis, you're not just "being there for them" — you're slowly breaking yourself down from the inside out.

Stress is expensive. It'll cost you years off your life. It'll keep you in the doctor's office while the same people you've been supporting are out here living stress-free — because you carried it for them.

Homespun Reality Check

Some of y'all bought Junior two cars before you bought yourself one. You've been babysitting your sister's kids every weekend for the last three years but haven't had a weekend to yourself since Obama's first term. You've been cashing out on your cousin's rent while your own roof needs fixing.

And for what? Junior wrecked both cars and is back riding the bus. Your sister never offers to keep your kids for even one night. Your cousin is three months behind again. You're breaking your back to keep other people's heads above water, but nobody's bringing you a life raft.

The truth is, that "ride or die" loyalty some of us brag about is just "die" if the people we're riding for never change.

Relationships Should Pour, Not Punish

Some of us are in romantic relationships with depreciable people and calling it love. But love without growth is bondage. If they can't celebrate your wins, protect your peace, or match your effort, you're teaching yourself to survive on crumbs while pretending it's a feast.

Grace is free; access is earned. If someone keeps showing you who they are but expects you to keep showing up at your best—that's exploitation, not intimacy.

Anything less than mutual growth is theft—of your time, your purpose, and you.

Stop Spending on What Won't Spend Back

This isn't just about relatives—it's about where our money goes, period. We shop at businesses that disrespect us, and worse, we keep investing in celebrities, influencers, and brands that profit off our culture while giving nothing back.

We'll buy every sneaker, every concert ticket, every beauty product, but when it's time for them to stand up for us—they're silent, or worse, they side with those against us. That's also investing in depreciable people.

Every dollar is a vote. Every like, every stream, every repost is an investment. If they don't support your growth or your people, they don't deserve your money, your energy, or your attention.

The History of Making Us Popular, Then Leaving Us Behind

The pattern is older than social media. Long before TikTok dances and sneaker collabs, white-owned industries built fortunes by taking what Black people made popular—then locking us out of the profit.

In the early 20th century, jazz and blues artists like Ma Rainey and Bessie Smith filled clubs and sold records that put entire record labels on the map, yet contracts left them in poverty.

White artists would re-record their songs, strip them of soul, and make ten times the money.

In sports, the Negro Leagues produced legends like Satchel Paige and Josh Gibson who drew huge crowds and revenue. Integration into Major League Baseball didn't just give Black players a chance—it dismantled Black-owned teams, stadiums, and economies. Jackie Robinson broke the color barrier, but the Black baseball business that thrived before him was gutted, and the profit went to white owners.

Fashion saw it too—Josephine Baker's Paris shows shaped couture trends, but the designers who copied her style rarely credited her. And in beauty, Madam C.J. Walker built a hair care empire in the early 1900s, only for white-owned beauty corporations to eventually dominate the shelves using formulas and marketing she pioneered.

Even in the modern era, we've seen hip-hop—born in the Bronx and nurtured by Black DJs and MCs—become a billion-dollar global industry where the largest record companies are not Black-owned. Streetwear brands built by Black creatives set trends that luxury fashion now mimics at ten times the price, without investing back into the communities that birthed them.

This is why supporting celebrities, brands, and businesses that don't pour back into us isn't harmless—it's history repeating itself. Every time we make someone rich who won't reinvest in our people, we help write the same story our grandparents watched play out. And that's a story we can't afford to keep telling.

You Were Called to Steward, Not Save

Fear keeps us in these cycles—fear of being alone, labeled disloyal, or called "too good." But maybe you are different, and that's not something to apologize for.

WHY YOU SHOULDN'T EAT FROM SOME WHITE PEOPLE

God didn't put vision in you to babysit dysfunction. Stop crucifying yourself for people who wouldn't carry a cross for you. Redirect that energy toward your own growth, future, and peace.

Because you can't build wealth, peace, or legacy by constantly rescuing people who choose not to grow.

Let Them Grow or Let Them Go

You don't owe anyone your ruin. You don't owe anyone your breakdown. You don't owe anyone your destiny. Let them grow—or let them go.

Next Steps

• **Stop bailing out grown people with repeat offenses.** If they keep going back to jail, debt, or drama—they're not learning. And you're not helping.

• **Redirect your support to those who are trying.** A niece going to college, a neighbor starting a side hustle, a teen with a vision—these are investments worth making.

• **Cut ties with users.** That includes the married man you're dating, the daughter who only calls when she needs something, or the boss who never sees your worth. Stop answering. Start healing.

• **Save something every check.** Even $5. Get a money order and put it somewhere hard to touch. Build your muscle for consistency.

• **Brand yourself as valuable.** Don't just expect people to see your worth—live like you know it.

- **Create community around purpose, not pity.** If your circle is full of people you have to carry, it's time to trade that circle for a ladder.

You don't owe anyone your ruin. You don't owe anyone your breakdown. You don't owe anyone your destiny.

Let them grow—or let them go.

WHY YOU SHOULDN'T EAT FROM SOME WHITE PEOPLE

🪶 Reflection & Growth

What truth on this page hit you the hardest?

_____

_____

_____

_____

How does it show up in your own life?

_____

_____

_____

_____

What one step will you take to shift it?

_____

_____

_____

_____

CHAPTER NINETEEN
EXTINCTION

"Politics and the racial environment [are] threatening the human family. But Black males, in particular, are endangered. Our attitudes, our ignorance, our savagery are all lending to a plan — a conspiracy to make the Black man, not endangered, but extinct. ... If God doesn't intervene, we will be extinct."
Minister Louis Farrakhan

Extinction

Extinction doesn't always mean the last breath is taken. Sometimes, it's the slow erosion of spirit, identity, memory, and will. We think of endangered species as wildlife disappearing from the earth, but cultures, legacies, and whole peoples can be endangered too. Black Americans aren't vanishing in the traditional sense, but we are living through a crisis of erosion—mental, spiritual, cultural, and generational. Not sudden death, but gradual disappearance.

We once roared with progress. After slavery, Black excellence soared: we built Greenwood, founded schools, voter leagues, fraternities, and newspapers. We survived Jim Crow, the Great Migration, and economic oppression—and still rose. Our ancestors didn't just endure; they created a cultural cosmos from chaos.

But now, too many of us survive without vision. We confuse trending with building, and presence with power.

Forbes and related forecasts show that, if current trends continue, median Black household wealth is projected to hit zero by 2053—while white household wealth continues to grow. That projected erosion isn't just a statistic—it's a forecast of extinction. Without systemic change and intentional community building, Black economic stability isn't just eroding—it's vanishing.

Eroding Foundations

Our schools are shrinking. Public education—once a ladder for Black advancement—is now starved: underfunded, disproportionately disciplinary, and suffering from teacher shortages. Many Black children attend schools with outdated materials, minimal tech, and little emotional or academic support. Black students consistently score lowest in reading proficiency, weakening the foundation for every other path forward.

Family structures are deteriorating. In 1960, 61% of Black adults were married; today, that number is below 30%. That drop signals not just a shift in norms—but a loss of partnership, structure, and generational planning.

We are also in the midst of a demographic crisis. The U.S. total fertility rate in 2023 was just 1.616 births per woman—well below the replacement level of about 21 Meanwhile, Black birthrates have declined, and maternal mortality remains alarmingly high. In 2023, Black women died at a rate of 50.3 per 100,000 live births—more than three times that of white women, who had a rate of 14.5. That is extinction in real time.

WHY YOU SHOULDN'T EAT FROM SOME WHITE PEOPLE

The Hijacking of Our Culture

Hip-hop started as resistance and liberation; now it's corporatized and sanitized. We created the sound; corporations took the royalties. Our creative genius fuels global industries, yet creators often die broke or silenced.

Social media and professional standards continue to penalize us for our culture. TikTok algorithms elevate other faces, while our expressions of identity—afros, braids, hoodies, sneakers—can still be suppressed. Our flavor is commodified, our presence policed. We're being duplicated, exploited, and erased.

As Jay-Z said: *"Until you own your own, you can't be free."* But too often, we're still renting everything—from our image to our identity.

Erosion of Institutions

HBCUs were once revolutionary spaces—protecting minds and elevating culture. Yet they remain chronically underfunded: lacking dorms, research facilities, and scholarships—while PWIs with fewer Black students receive far greater donations

Meanwhile, Black studies programs are being cut and Black history is banned in schools across multiple states. Book bans and censorship aren't education—they're erasure. Silence here is complicity.

Civil Rights in Reverse

The Voting Rights Act of 1965 was gutted in 2013, triggering a wave of voter suppression via strict ID laws, polling place closures, and strategic gerrymandering. Under the Trump administration, civil rights enforcement weakened, police reform stalled, and accountability measures were rolled back—impacting housing, employment, healthcare, and education.

These policies roll back generations of progress. And yet many of us remain distracted, captivated by culture rather than critical issues. Ignoring extinction only accelerates it.

Breakdown of Relationship and Trust

We're divided by stereotypes and untreated wounds. Gender dynamics became battlegrounds, not bridges. Declining marriage is not just about romance—it's about losing trust, legacy, and financial stability.

Too often, boundary-setting becomes avoidance. We survive love instead of creating it. Extinction is relational: when a people can't connect, they vanish. Relationships carry economic, cultural, and spiritual infrastructure. When those collapse, so does the future.

Spiritual Shrinking

Black spirituality held us through storms—from hush harbors to civil rights pulpits. But many sacred spaces have traded prophetism for performance. We're more spiritual yet more disconnected—scrolling for crystals, praying for what we won't plan for.

When sacred community dissolves, sacred accountability vanishes. And when the collective soul is exhausted, nothing else can be restored.

Economic Starvation

We have over $1.7 trillion in buying power, yet less than 2% of businesses in the U.S. are Black-owned. We were taught to consume—not compound. Without access to capital, land, and finance, we remain dependent on systems that exploit us.

WHY YOU SHOULDN'T EAT FROM SOME WHITE PEOPLE

Predatory industries—from payday loans to rent-to-own stores—stalk our communities precisely because we are underserved. Wealth is protection. Without it, extinction is engineered.

Distractions and the Myth of Progress

Visibility isn't power. One billionaire, one politician, or one TV face doesn't uplift millions still struggling. Representation can pacify by creating the illusion of progress, while communities decay.

We've lost over 90% of Black-owned farms in a century. Gentrification is sweeping out our neighborhoods. Progress without rooted protection is illusion.

Generational Disruption

Our survival blueprint passed through griots and grandmother lines. Now that bridge is broken. Elders dismissed; tradition mocked. Our children are raised more by devices than discipline. They inherit trauma but not tools, pain without preparation.

We binge instead of build, scroll instead of study, like instead of lead. If we don't reconnect the past and the future, we become ghosts in our own lineage.

This Is the Warning—Not the Eulogy

Extinction is a pattern—not a prophecy—and patterns can be broken. We must reawaken our hunger to learn, organize, love with discipline, and build with unapologetic purpose. Blackness is not a burden—it's a blueprint for resilience and collective power.

We are not powerless—just distracted and disconnected. Revival demands plans, purpose, and unity. Time is short, but our fight is righteous.

Tools for Revival: Reversing the Decline

We are not powerless. We've just been distracted, divided, and discouraged. But Black people have never needed ideal conditions to do extraordinary things. What we need now is not more performance—but more plans. Not just more pride—but more purpose. Revival is possible, but it must be strategic. Here are tools we must begin using—today:

1. Rebuild the Black Family Intentionally.
Whether through marriage, co-parenting, or chosen kinship, we must normalize commitment, communication, and consistency. Prioritize healthy love, not just passion. Teach children legacy, not just loyalty. Family is more than a bond—it's a foundation.

2. Invest in Financial Education & Ownership.
Start money conversations early. Create community investment clubs. Support Black-owned banks. Learn about trusts, insurance, and estate planning. Buying power is not enough—build ownership. Wealth is protection in a world that often targets us.

3. Fight for Educational Sovereignty.
Don't just depend on schools. Create reading groups. Demand culturally relevant curriculums. Support HBCUs and create scholarships. Literacy and comprehension are our first lines of defense against misinformation and manipulation.

4. Heal the Disconnect.
Black men and women must choose healing over hostility. Attend therapy. Host roundtables. Read books that foster emotional intelligence. We are not enemies—we are extensions of each other. Our healing is generational work.

5. Protect Our Creative Legacy.
Support Black creators. Demand ownership rights in music, film,

fashion, and media. Teach young artists business basics. We are not just the talent—we are the architects.

6. Reclaim Faith as a Tool of Resistance.
Whether in church, mosque, temple, or sacred stillness—return to discipline. Pray. Plan. Practice what our ancestors died to protect. Faith without action is extinction in disguise.

7. Get Politically Local.
National elections matter, but local decisions shape schools, policing, housing, and health access. Attend city council meetings. Email your representatives. Organize voter drives. Don't wait until something goes wrong—vote before it does.

8. Don't Just Build—Document.
Write your family history. Archive photos. Record elders. Our erasure starts with forgetfulness. Memory is resistance. Legacy is a form of literacy.

We are not the end. We are the remnant. The seed. The signal. The survivors. But if we want to remain more than that—if we want to thrive—we must act like a people who know the value of their existence.

This is not our funeral. This is our fight.

🪶 Reflection & Growth

If you did nothing with this truth, what would your life look like in 5 years?

_____
_____
_____
_____

If you acted on it, what could your life look like?

_____
_____
_____
_____

What's the first action that bridges you from here to there?

_____
_____
_____
_____

NOTES

- Alexander, M. (2010). *The New Jim Crow: Mass Incarceration in the Age of Colorblindness.* The New Press.
- DuBois, W. E. B. (1903). *The Souls of Black Folk.* A.C. McClurg & Co.
- hooks, bell. (2000). *All About Love: New Visions.* William Morrow.
- Kendi, I. X. (2019). *How to Be an Antiracist.* One World.
- Malcolm X. (1963). "Message to the Grassroots."
- Muhammad, K. G. (2010). *The Condemnation of Blackness: Race, Crime, and the Making of Modern Urban America.* Harvard University Press.
- Browder, A. T. (1992). *Nile Valley Contributions to Civilization: Exploding the Myths.* Institute of Karmic Guidance.
- Browder, A. T. (1996). *From the Browder File: 22 Essays on the African American Experience.* Institute of Karmic Guidance.
- Thiong'o, N. W. (1986). *Decolonising the Mind: The Politics of Language in African Literature.* James Currey Ltd.
- Achebe, C. (1958). *Things Fall Apart.* Heinemann.
- U.S. Securities and Exchange Commission. (2023, January 25). *Accredited investors.* https://www.sec.gov/education/capitalraising/building-blocks/accredited-investor
- Centers for Disease Control and Prevention. (2022). *Black or African American Populations.* Retrieved from https://www.cdc.gov
- National Center for Education Statistics. (2023). *NAEP Reading Assessments.* https://nces.ed.gov/nationsreportcard
- U.S. Census Bureau. (2022). *Income and Poverty in the United States: 2021.* https://www.census.gov

- U.S. Department of Justice. (2021). *Prisoners in 2020.* Bureau of Justice Statistics. https://bjs.ojp.gov
- ims, M., Diez-Roux, A. V., Gebreab, S. Y., et al. (2016). *Perceived discrimination and hypertension among African Americans in the Jackson Heart Study.* American Journal of Public Health, 106(5), 896–902. https://doi.org/10.2105/AJPH.2015.302985
- Geronimus, A. T., Hicken, M., Keene, D., & Bound, J. (2006). *"Weathering" and age patterns of allostatic load scores among blacks and whites in the United States.* American Journal of Public Health, 96(5), 826–833. https://doi.org/10.2105/AJPH.2004.060749
- Pew Research Center. (2022, February 16). *Interracial marriage: Who is "marrying out"?* Retrieved from https://www.pewresearch.org
- McKinsey & Company. (2021). *The Economic State of Black America.* https://www.mckinsey.com
- Forbes. (2023). *Black Women and the Wealth Gap: What the Data Tells Us.* https://www.forbes.com
- Pew Research Center. (2022). *Marriage and Cohabitation in the U.S.* https://www.pewresearch.org
- *Black Twitter: A People's History* (2024). [Amazon Prime Video].
- *The 1619 Project* (2023). [Hulu].
- *New Jack City* (1991). Directed by Mario Van Peebles.
- *The Color Purple* (1985). Directed by Steven Spielberg.
- *Hidden Figures* (2016). Directed by Theodore Melfi.
- Banner, D. (n.d.). Community commentary, Charleston, SC forum.
- Umar Johnson. (n.d.). Public commentary on Black male mentorship and cultural healing.
- Jesse Williams. (2016). BET Humanitarian Speech.
- Toni Morrison. (1993). Nobel Prize Lecture.
- Carter G. Woodson. (1933). *The Mis-Education of the Negro.*
- Nkrumah, K. (n.d.). *I am not African because I was born in Africa, but because Africa was born in me.*

- [Quote attributed widely across Pan-African literature.]
- African Proverb. (n.d.). *Until the lion tells his side of the story, the tale of the hunt will always glorify the hunter.* [Traditional oral proverb.]
- African Proverb. (n.d.). *When the roots are deep, there is no reason to fear the wind.* [Traditional oral proverb.]
- Lacks, H. (Referenced). Immortal cell contributions. See: Skloot, R. (2010). *The Immortal Life of Henrietta Lacks.*
- Greenwood, Tulsa. (1921). Referenced in *Black Wall Street* history.
- Gullah Geechee Cultural Heritage Corridor Commission. (n.d.). https://gullahgeecheecorridor.org
- Anderson, C. (1994). *Black labor, white wealth: The search for power and economic justice.* PowerNomics Corporation of America.
- Baldwin, J. (1963). *The fire next time.* Vintage International.
- Cecelski, D. S., & Tyson, T. B. (Eds.). (1998). *Democracy betrayed: The Wilmington race riot of 1898 and its legacy.* University of North Carolina Press.
- Green, M. (Creator). (2020, August 16). *Lovecraft Country* [TV series episode]. In M. Green (Executive Producer), *Lovecraft Country*. HBO.
- hooks, b. (1992). *Black looks: Race and representation.* South End Press.
- Johnson, H. B. (1998). *Black Wall Street: From riot to renaissance in Tulsa's historic Greenwood District.* Eakin Press.
- Madigan, T. (2001). *The burning: Massacre, destruction, and the Tulsa race riot of 1921.* Thomas Dunne Books.
- Manly, A. (1898, August). Editorial. *The Daily Record* (Wilmington, NC). Quoted in Zucchino, D. (2020). *Wilmington's lie: The murderous coup of 1898 and the rise of white supremacy* (pp. 175–176). Atlantic Monthly Press.

- Nielsen, L. B. (2004). *License to harass: Law, hierarchy, and offensive public speech.* Princeton University Press.
- Touré, J. (2015, April). The hidden cost of integration. *The Root.* https://www.theroot.com
  - Brookings Institution. (2024, January 30). *Black wealth is increasing—but so is the racial wealth gap.* Brookings.
  - Fortune Editors. (2024, February 9). *There are now more Black CEOs in the Fortune 500 than ever before—but it's still only 1.6%.* Fortune.
  - Group Black. (2024). *The Black Creator Economy: 2024 Black creator research report.*
  - Nielsen. (2025, February). *Engaging Black audiences: A deep dive into consumer behavior and media influence.* Nielsen.
  - Pew Research Center. (2023, December 4). *Wealth gaps across racial and ethnic groups in the United States.* Pew Research Center.
  - Reuters. (2025, January 6). *Boardroom diversity stalls in the face of conservative backlash.* Reuters
  - • Zucchino, D. (2020). *Wilmington's lie: The murderous coup of 1898 and the rise of white supremacy.* AtlanticCROWN Act. (2020). Legislation banning hair-based discrimination.CDC. (2023). *Obesity and African American Women.* https://www.cdc.gov/obesityNational Assessment of Educational Progress (NAEP). (2023). *Reading and Math Scores for Black Students.*
  - American Psychological Association. (2022). *The impact of literacy on mental health and social mobility.*
  - Nkrumah, K. (n.d.). *I am not African because I was born in Africa, but because Africa was born in me.* [Quote attributed widely across Pan-African literature.]

- Bryant, J. H. (2014). *How the Poor Can Save Capitalism: Rebuilding the Path to the Middle Class.* Berrett-Koehler Publishers.
- African Proverb. (n.d.). *Until the lion tells his side of the story, the tale of the hunt will always glorify the hunter.* [Traditional oral proverb.]
- African Proverb. (n.d.). *When the roots are deep, there is no reason to fear the wind.* [Traditional oral proverb.]
- World Bank. (2023). *Global Economic Prospects – Africa overview.* https://www.worldbank.org/en/publication/global-economic-prospects
- International Monetary Fund (IMF). (2023). *Sub-Saharan Africa Regional Economic Outlook.* https://www.imf.org/en/Publications/REO/SSA
- African Development Bank Group. (2023). *Africa's Macroeconomic Performance and Outlook 2023.* https://www.afdb.org/en/documents
- NielsenIQ. (2023). *The Power of the Black Consumer Report.* https://www.nielseniq.com/global/en/insights/
- China Africa Research Initiative (CARI). (2021). *Chinese Loans to Africa Database.* Johns Hopkins University, SAIS. https://chinaafricaresearchinitiative.org
- Anderson, E. (2018, Nov 1). *The Business of Black Beauty: Who Really Profits?* Essence Magazine. https://www.essence.com
- Abdullahi, A. (2022). *Shea Butter Supply Chains and African Export Disparities. Journal of African Trade, 9*(2), 63–78. https://doi.org/10.1016/j.jafr.2022.04.005
- CNN. (2019, Dec 27). *Year of Return: Ghana's campaign to reconnect the African diaspora.*

https://www.cnn.com/travel/article/ghana-year-of-return-diaspora/index.html
- BBC News Africa. (2022, Jan 20). *Why African Americans Are Moving to Africa.* https://www.bbc.com/news/world-africa
- Rodgers, R. (2021). *We Should All Be Millionaires: A Woman's Guide to Earning More, Building Wealth, and Gaining Economic Power.* HarperCollins Leadership.

WHY YOU SHOULDN'T EAT FROM SOME WHITE PEOPLE

Thank You.

Whew. You made it.

And I don't just mean to the end of the book—I mean through the parts that poked you, called you out, called you higher, made you cuss at me and reminded you who you are. That's no small thing. That's *everything*.

So let me say this plain:
Thank you. For reading. For feeling. For staying. For not skipping the hard parts. For letting my truth crack something open in you.

This ain't just pages and paper. This was a mirror, a megaphone, and a map. And now that you've seen some things, felt some things, named some things—*you can't unsee it.*

And that's good. Because now it's on you.

To show up better.
To set some boundaries.
To love with more intention.
To stop playing small in rooms you were built to lead in.
To stop watering dead plants and call it "loyalty."
To be the one in your family that says, *"Not this time. Not no more."*

This world gon' keep spinning. But now that you got some new tools in your bag, how you spin with it is up to you.

I wrote this with love. With truth. With urgency.
You read it with grace. With fire. With spirit.

I see you. I honor you. I'm rooting for you.

Now go be the light they hoped for.
Go be the one they feared you'd become.

With a whole lotta love and even more accountability,
— **Veronica Pearson**
Your sister in truth, legacy, and doing the most… on purpose.

Affirmation:
I'm the shift my people been waiting on. I don't just break chains—I build tables, open doors, and leave 'em unlocked.

Mic drop. Veronica out.

Let's Stay Connected

You didn't just finish a book. You just stepped into a movement.

And the next step? *Connection.*

I don't do this just to talk—I do this to build. And if something in these pages woke something up in you, don't let that fire die down. Stay in touch. Stay plugged in. Let's get to work.

Why Stay Connected?

Because we're not meant to build alone.
Because you might need a strategy, a partner, a push—or a reminder.
Because when you connect with builders, you remember you're one too.

I've created platforms, events, content, and spaces to help people like you move from ideas to impact. Whether it's media, mindset, property, purpose, or partnerships—I've walked the road and I've helped others pave theirs too.

You're not behind. You're just getting started.

Ways to Reach Me

Website: **www.dammimedia.com**
Instagram & Tiktok: @**veronicaresponds**
Podcast: **Why You Shouldn't with Veronica**
YouTube: @**Dammimedia**
Bookings & Collabs: **connect@dammimedia.com**

www.ingramcontent.com/pod-product-compliance
Lightning Source LLC
Chambersburg PA
CBHW072003290426
44109CB00018B/2120